I MARRIED A
THRILL-SEEKER

I MARRIED A THRILL-SEEKER

A Cautious Wife's Memoir of Her Husband's Risk-Taking and Their Long Road to Recovery

DANIELLE KAPLAN

RE:BOOKS

www.rebooks.ca

Published in Canada by RE:BOOKS.

RE:BOOKS
380 Macpherson Ave. Suite 306
Toronto ON
M4V 3E3
www.rebooks.ca

Content warning: motorcycle accident, hospitalization, trauma, medical trauma, PTSD, motor vehicle accidents, death

First RE:BOOKS Edition:

ISBN: 978-1-7386702-0-8
eBook ISBN: 978-1-7386702-1-5

RE:BOOKS and all associated logos are trademarks and/or registered marks of RE:BOOKS.

Library and Archives Canada Cataloguing in Publication
Title: I married a thrill seeker : a cautious wife's memoir of her husband's risk-taking and their long road to recovery / Danielle Kaplan.
Names: Kaplan, Danielle, author.
Identifiers: Canadiana (print) 2022041176X | Canadiana (ebook) 20220412383 | ISBN 9781738670208 (softcover) | ISBN 9781738670215 (ebook)
Subjects: LCSH: Kaplan, Danielle. | LCSH: Kaplan, Danielle—Marriage. | LCSH: Kaplan, Danielle—Family. | LCSH: Traffic accident victims—Family relationships. | LCSH: Motorcycling injuries. | LCSH: Wives—Canada—Biography. | LCGFT: Autobiographies.
Classification: LCC HE5614.5.C2 K37 2022 | DDC 363.12/5092—dc23
Printed and bound in Canada.
1 3 5 7 9 10 8 6 4 2

Cover design by: Jordan Lunn
Typesetting by: Karl Hunt
Author photo: Josh Kaplan
Interior images: Danielle Kaplan

Contents

To my mom, my dad, and the powerful life lessons you taught me.

Prologue

M Y HUSBAND STEVE is a free spirit. Heading out alone on a motorcycle for weeks at a time was his passion. He had been riding for five years, from the time our kids were fifteen and twelve years old. We have been married for twenty-seven years, and at fifty, I felt wiser, stronger and living my best life. But the riding was causing friction in our lives. Neither of us could deny that.

"Why would you go to the Yukon and Alaska alone on a motorbike?" I asked.

Steve replied, "Because I have the opportunity. You know I love riding solo and exploring the wilderness of British Columbia, Yukon, and Alaska. Why not?"

This wasn't an unreasonable question. After all, what man would choose to risk his life, driving so far, so fast, that it might not just impact him but his whole family? Why would anyone ignore the danger signs and drive over five hundred kilometres on a seldom-used, wet gravel road with no one in sight?

It wasn't my choice and there was no way I could stop him. For many years, he chose his bike and his extreme rides over everything else. In a sense, it's like living with an addict. I couldn't rationalize with him or talk him out of seeking his next high. Believe me, I tried. Although our children Josh and Gabi thought this trip was insane, they accepted their dad's need for challenges; they accepted his excessive nature.

Steve was no weekend-warrior Harley-Davidson–type, despite having Harley friends. Harley-Davidson bikes are more the basic cruiser for urban and extended weekend road trips. Steve has a BMW R1200GS Enduro, an adventure bike, specifically for off-road biking and epic motorcycle road trips. It's the same motorcycle Ewan McGregor and Charley Boorman rode on their trips from London to New York and Scotland to Cape Agulhas in South Africa. This was no lightweight motorcycle, with its place of honour in our garage. This motorcycle is his love and lone companion as he navigated unfamiliar territory. He was an adventurer with an iron butt—or at least he was trying to be.

Steve belonged to the Iron Butt Association, an organization of thousands of riders globally dedicated to "safe" long-distance motorcycle riding. As the name suggests, the guidelines and goals are to cover a great deal of distance in an absurdly short time. Steve completed their most popular ride, the SaddleSore 1000 challenge, which was sixteen hundred kilometres within twenty-four hours, and the Bun Burner 1500, which was twenty-four hundred kilometres in less than thirty-six hours to obtain his ride certificates. He felt that this was good preparation for his first trip to Alaska. He also rode the Great Lakes Gold, covering almost four thousand kilometres around the five Great Lakes in under fifty hours. He napped briefly and ate while stopping for gas. He was so proud of this accomplishment. But I believe this takes craziness on two wheels to a whole other level. In my mind, his five trips spread across numerous summer weekends were ridiculously unsafe and risky. I understood his dream to cover distance, cross the country, and explore the beautiful terrain on the open road. But this? This was hard core.

Steve thrives on thrill and adventure, the desire to push the limits— these are all characteristics of his sensation-seeking personality. He was always up for a challenge in work and in play. Me? I walk the moderate, cautious, and restrained road. On the outside, Steve is calm, serious, and level-headed, as his work in finance presents. But deep below the surface, he is drawn to risk, is spontaneous, and shows no fear. Living with him makes for a bumpy ride because a man like Steve rarely weighs his actions against his consequences.

Steve knew the danger in riding motorcycles. Although he was unprotected, with no roll bars or airbags, he loved being exposed to the elements. The rain, wind, smells, stones, wild animals, tight corners, and dusty roads all appealed to his sense of adventure.

After completing many safety courses, including off road and track driving, he believed that he was an extremely safe rider—and an invincible one. He always said it was only the other people and vehicles on the road he had to watch out for. He never looked within and never questioned if he was pushing his luck or his behaviour too far.

On July 1, 2011, Steve left for his latest—and unknowingly last—journey. The year before, we had been to see a marriage counsellor over the tension his motorbike was creating between us. When we first met, he had a scrambler/dirt bike for off road riding. To appease me and my concerns he sold it. When he "spontaneously" bought his BMW Enduro, I was quite upset to say the least. He assured me I had nothing to worry about. At university, I had studied brain injury communication after motorcycle accidents and couldn't believe that now my grown-up husband owned one.

Over time I just couldn't cope with his extreme riding any longer. It was clear, at least to me, that his motorbike was his other wife. She wasn't going anywhere, except on long rides to interesting places, with Steve in her saddle. I wasn't going anywhere; my priority was my family and the stability we could offer our children. Josh is twenty and studying film production at a university in Montreal. Gabi is seventeen and in her final grade of high school. My parents, Steve's sister, and my brother-in-law were all opposed to Steve having a motorcycle, let alone these long-distance solo adventures. Following my master's research in brain injury, I had worked in acute care hospitals for twenty-five years as a speech-language pathologist in the field of brain and spinal injury. I was quite familiar with the consequences of high-risk adventure and extreme sports.

The takeaway from our counselling sessions was that Steve needed to show more empathy and consider my increasing anxiety about his zeal for motorcycling. I needed to express more interest in his passion for riding, encourage him, and validate his accomplishments. Fair or not, we were at the crossroads. We agreed to work hard at better understanding each other to reduce the stress in our relationship. But little changed. Steve couldn't give up his motorcycling and I couldn't grow comfortable with his risky behaviour.

Perhaps I should have given him an ultimatum—the bike or me—but I never did. It's not my nature to do so. I knew how important the adventures were to him. And I loved him (and still do). Despite my reservations, I chose to accept and support him. He's been my best friend, and my family, "my person," since I was nineteen years old.

In hindsight, we were foolish and short-sighted. What lay ahead would change our lives forever.

CHAPTER 1

Two weeks before the Canada Day trip (July 11, 2011)

"IF YOU HAVE a frickin' spinal injury, or a head injury, or you die on this trip, I'm going to kill you first! If you think you're going to leave me to manage our lives, the kids, and the house without you, you are so wrong. Do *not* get hurt or die on this trip!"

These are my parting words to my husband Steve before he set off on his latest adventure that morning. Although he had five years of long-distance motorcycle riding behind him, I have never said *that* to him before. Naturally, I have thought it several times, but I have never expressed my fears or my resentment so bluntly.

How prophetic my words turn out to be. I suppose I never should have said them. Instead, I should have smiled and encouraged him as I have in the past. But I am exhausted and feeling fragile as I wrote an exam last night and was unsure of my results. Perhaps sleep deprivation and anxiety are inhibiting my ability to filter my thoughts. Or maybe I am finally being honest. I am scared, and I can't hold it in.

Steve laughs. "Dans, what a terrible way to send me off. I promise you I'm going to be fine. I always am. I promise you that I am going to come back in one piece. You'll see me soon."

I laugh along with him, but I repeat my ominous warning. I can't bear to think of him hurt. Trauma is something I'm all too familiar with. While I'm no longer practising, I spent years working in hospitals with spine- and brain-injured patients as a speech pathologist. I've been in critical care wards, on the spinal floor, and on the trauma unit. I've seen it all—what's possible, what's probable, and what stems from the consequences of risky behaviour. Yet, where I see risk, all Steve sees is reward—the thrill of the open road, the freedom of the air all around him, the wildness of the places he'll see.

I bought a small gift for Steve to take with him—a leather bracelet with a stone bearing an evil eye. It is meant to be a lighthearted parting gift, but when I give it to him, I ask him to wear it and not take it off until he comes home safely. I joke that the evil eye is me watching over him, keeping him safe. To placate me, he reluctantly puts it on.

This gift is atypical for both of us. Steve never wears jewellery and I never buy any for him. At the time, I am not thinking of folklore, superstitions, or legends. I don't believe in karma or the power of spiritual belief; I believe in science, coincidence, and timing. It is only years later that I learn some Irish, Mediterranean, and Asian cultures believe receiving the evil eye will cause misfortune or injury. In hindsight, I wish I had known that when I bought the bracelet.

As Steve is about to leave, I take a few parting pictures. He looks strong and excited on his large BMW. We laugh, embrace, and then I watch my invincible man ride his macho motorcycle down the street. Waiting until he turns the corner, until I can no longer hear the noise of his bike, I stare after the empty road. I should go inside, instead; I stand on the street in my pajamas for a few minutes longer. Tired. It is now six-thirty am. Reluctantly, I retreat into my empty home, climb into my cozy white bed, and fall into a peaceful, much-needed sleep.

I wake a few hours later, feeling rested and a little less stressed. I've been studying for months to get my certification as a personal trainer, and Steve waited until the day after my exam to leave. This considerate act speaks to a more thoughtful side of my husband, in contrast with the rugged free spirit who's been raring to get on the road.

Steve, too, values the nature of education and experience. He has taken many training courses and has thousands of kilometres under his belt. This is to be his second-round trip from Toronto to Alaska, exploring parts of the Northern United States and Western Canada. He enjoys travelling solo, riding at his own pace, setting his own timetable, taking photographs, and enjoying the tranquillity. It is a world away from his everyday life, working in a high-stress corporate finance office.

His plan is to cover just over sixteen thousand kilometres in twenty-one days. It's no small undertaking and he's been preparing for months. Researching maps, the terrain, routes, famed sites, and scenic roads, he knows where he can fill up with gas and where to stay overnight. His bike is equipped with all the latest gear designed to make the ride safer and more comfortable. He always travels with a SPOT, a GPS transmitter, which relays his location to a website where friends and family can follow his route. This is how I know he's safe; it helps alleviate some of the stress I feel about his trips.

The SPOT is set to automatically email me with his coordinates every time he stops. It also has an emergency button, which, when pressed, will connect to an Emergency Response Centre in Texas. It is reassuring to know where he is and whether he is moving or stopped. I breathe easier when I receive his messages, phone calls, and emails.

Prior to Steve's departure, he sends this message to his colleagues, friends, and family:

> *If you feel bored and have nothing better to do, you can follow me on my Alaskan journey. The plan is to leave Toronto on Friday July 1 and return on the 24th, while working some days along the way.*

Among the many replies, this one stands out:

> *U are one crazy mother f . . .*
> *Would love to but am chained to my desk*
> *Enjoy.*

With Steve gone, and our children Josh and Gabi working as counsellors at an overnight camp, I am alone. Looking forward to having three weeks to myself to enjoy my own space and unwind, I plan to teach Pilates classes at my studio, travel to our family lakefront cottage, and visit with friends and my parents—savouring that rarest of treasures for a working mom, time to myself.

As with any of his last trips, I know Steve will keep contact as often as he can. When he has cell reception, he'll call me daily to say hello and update me on his adventures. When he is out of phone range, he'll email to describe his day. Whenever he travels, I keep all his voicemails, emails, and text messages, only deleting them when he returns home. I do the same thing when my children or parents travel without me. I suppose it's one of my obsessive behaviours. I feel that if I have the message, I am keeping part of my family member with me, should anything happen.

Six months later, after this fateful day, I realize that I still have all of Steve's voicemail messages.

Hey Dans it's me. Umm, my GPS has broken down, so I might have to get a new one as I get to a bigger city. My phone charger is not working at the moment, so I'm gonna run out of phone pretty soon. But my SPOT is working, so you will get the texts from me that I'm fine. Everything is going really well. It's pretty hot here . . . 30 degrees. I'm headed towards Mackinaw Bridge. Speak to you later. Bye.

Hi Dans, it's me. I just stopped in Anchorage to get some earphones. My other ones broke. I'm actually having a good trip here (laughing) even with everything breaking. But anyhow, I'll call you later. I'm continuing on my way to Fairbanks. Speak to you soon. Bye.

I don't recall Steve having so many problems with technical gadgets on previous trips; however, he seems to be sorting things out and taking matters in stride. I'm not surprised. He's always been one to handle challenges as they come. This trip, more than any other, will put these abilities to the test.

Over the course of his first few days on the road, he sends me a series of stunning photographs. Through his lens, he shares the mountains, glaciers, brown bears, and fascinating local people along his route. The descriptive prose in his emails is a lovely surprise, since it comes from a man of few words. This is his email from July 8, 2011:

Behind schedule, but who cares. I'm not going to rush things and also need to do work . . . but cold here today, so not a bad day to stay in and work! Sitting in a bar in Hyder, Alaska working on the budgets and watching bears strolling through the town. Not too shabby a way to work on unappealing numbers . . . Went on a great 50k ride to see the nearby glacier. It's been the best few weeks, just like last time. The scenery has been amazing, because it's so rugged and untouched in this part of the world. Massive snow-capped mountain ranges, wild animals and open expanse of forest, lakes and rivers. Went there also last time. It's nice going to places that I've seen before, as it's more familiar.

On July 14, he sends me another email, this time from Dawson City:

Hi Dans,

End of the day's ride and I stayed in this hole in the wall called Carmacks. I should have had my head read, but the weary dusty traveller needed a shower and some food. Had a shower but was too late for supper. Have an easy day and spent most of the time in Dawson City. The buildings in Dawson have been preserved so that they reflect the Gold rush era. Had a good massage at the Downtown Hotel from the Inn Keeper's daughter. There's a music festival here this weekend, so I'm going to stay here for Friday night as well. The border crossing for the route that I came to Dawson City, closes at 6:00 pm and I made it by 2 minutes . . .

I'm so sad, because leaving Fairbanks this morning is the return trip back home. Although there are still lots of places to still go to on the way home . . . Anyways, unfortunately my adventure is coming to an end soon, but I guess there are still other places to explore. I don't think anything can compare with the rugged natural beauty of Alaska, Yukon and BC, when I get there. Despite all the small things that have gone wrong, like the GPS breaking down, my riding glasses arm breaking off, the earphones . . . the bike has been perfect. It needs a good cleaning up when it gets home. It's been amazing again on the sand, mud roads and through all the construction areas. All the things I have for the bike, has made it easy to ride 1,000 km days and not feel tired at the end.

Have a fun weekend at the cottage.

Steve

This is the last email I receive, the day before his accident.

Clearly, he's enjoying his ride. But my emotions are mixed. Strangely, I've been worried about him for weeks; yet, suddenly, I feel bad for him. His adventure is ending and I know how much he loves to travel, see, and appreciate the beauty of the wilderness, and feel the wind on his face. My emotions are deeply conflicting—it isn't the time apart that I find hard but, rather, my concern for Steve's safety. I am self-sufficient (maybe too much for my own good) and love lazy days at the cottage with my girlfriends and parents. But still, I worry.

When we met, I was nineteen and he was twenty-three. Four years later, we married. We've shared so many experiences together: falling in love, immigrating to Canada, raising a family. Things would have been different a few years earlier when the kids were younger, and I was working at the hospital and trying to balance everything. I would have resented Steve, having to shoulder the family and household responsibilities while he followed his passion. But now that we're older, and Josh and Gabi are more independent, we do relish some time alone.

Still, these trips are long, and I am anxious. I appear to be coping better than I am. The trip's impact on me is far more than I let on. I try to put on a brave face, encouraging Steve's free spirit, yet I am really overwhelmed with it all.

Even though Steve regularly contacts me from the road, he doesn't realize that his messages create stress for me—comparing the most recent message to the previous one, making sure his coordinates are changing. This way, I know that he is on the move and not stuck somewhere. Each evening, he sends a final SPOT message announcing that he is stopping for the night and going to be stationary. Only then do I relax and leave my worries for the following day.

I guess I'm not cut out to be the wife of an extreme risk taker/adventurer.

CHAPTER 2

The day, the accident

SATURDAY JULY 16, 2011—the day our lives change forever. I've been spending a few days with my girlfriend at our cottage on the lake, a place of peace and tranquillity for me. When I awake, I lie in bed and stare out at the calm water, lush trees, and stunning blue sky. Everything feels so peaceful, holding the promise of another perfect cottage day. This is the calm before the storm.

My girlfriend leaves early in the morning and Steve's sister Maxine drives up with my nieces to enjoy a day in the sun. We are a close family and love spending time together, eating, talking, and tanning on the deck overlooking the water. My parents arrive later in the afternoon and plan to stay the night. Maxine and the girls enjoy a delicious dinner with us and then return to the city.

My parents, who are passionate about watching the news, particularly the BBC, want to catch up on the day's events, but we haven't hooked up the satellite TV yet this summer. I haven't missed it at all. My parents, however, are thrown by not being able to get their news fix.

I have a few light "chick flick" movies and subject my intellectual parents to the plight of Reese Witherspoon's character in *Legally Blonde 2: Red, White & Blonde*. We lean back on the cozy couches to watch the movie together. My parents struggle to stay awake. My mom, who always shoots straight, says she wishes something would happen so that the movie would come to an end. If only she knew how accurate her words would prove to be.

Ten minutes later, around nine pm, my cell phone rings. I pause the movie, thinking it must be Steve calling to say goodnight. I last spoke to him earlier this morning. I am eager to hear about his day and ensure that he is safe.

We have all heard about "the call." When I used to work at the hospital, my patients' families would speak about it; it's the moment your life changes forever. There is no going back. You cannot change the past and you cannot rewrite the story, no matter how much you wish you could.

A female voice introduces herself as Kelly and tells me she's calling from the International Emergency Response Coordination Center in Texas. It takes me a few seconds to process the information before my anxiety sets in. She asks to speak to either Stephen or Danielle K. This is really happening.

When I identify myself, she tells me that she is monitoring Steve's SPOT device and that they have received an emergency activation signal. I ask her exactly what that means. She believes someone activated the system and then reactivated it a few minutes later. She asks me who is using the SPOT device and whether she should send out emergency services. She adds that the coordinates indicate a very remote area in the Yukon. I tell her to dispatch the first responders.

She repeats that the signal has come from an extremely remote region. Although I am stunned, I remain calm and try to think logically. She asks for a description of Steve, the bike, and the clothing he is wearing. She also wants to know if he is white, Black, or another race. I think this is an odd question. It bothers me that it's necessary to ask about his race. Under these stressful circumstances, I become distracted by my politically correct nature. What difference does his race make? How many crazy individuals would be on a motorcycle in the remote parts of Yukon? Will they really confuse him with someone else?

Really, they just need his description. I tell her about his motorcycle, his outer clothing, and the colour of his helmet. My parents, realizing that the call is about Steve, hover around me. Somehow, I'm still thinking clearly, despite the circumstances. I have always been someone who copes well in crisis; now my capacity is about to be put to the test.

I ask Kelly whether Steve's coordinates have changed or if the bike is stationary. She replies that the bike is not moving, and it has not moved for at least twenty minutes. My heart pounds. Kelly has requested all emergency services, but it will take at least two to three hours for them to reach him. She tells me an ambulance and the RCMP (Royal Canadian Mounted Police) are on their way. My stomach roils. Despite being scared, I don't want to frighten my parents. I fill them in as calmly as possible and then I phone Michael, Steve's brother who lives in Toronto.

Michael leaves the party he is attending and rushes home to check Steve's website to track his location. We take turns calling the SPOT Emergency Response Center, talking to the two operators. They seem well trained but have little to tell us beyond what we already know.

I am now operating on autopilot. My parents and I decide to close the cottage and head back to Toronto. It takes us half an hour to clear the boathouse deck, shut the windows, and empty the fridge. Although I don't realize it yet, it will be a long time before I return to the cottage on the lake that I love so much—my little piece of heaven.

My mom and my dog Maddy accompany me in my car, while my dad follows behind. Maddy, the sweetest golden retriever, is really Steve's dog. They just adore each other. I have a brief shocking thought. What if . . . the worse has happened? Amidst all the chaos, my thoughts are how Maddy will cope.

It is now ten-thirty and dark outside. We're in cottage country, on quiet roads with few lights. My dad isn't a great night driver, so I drive much slower than I normally would, even though I'm eager to get to the city.

Michael, who is in touch with the Response Center, calls me in the car to update me. At around eleven-thirty, we learn the RCMP are ten to fifteen minutes from Steve's location. My heart feels like it's sitting in my throat. I know nothing about Steve's condition. Is he injured? How badly? Is he even alive?

I tell my mom that when the responders reach Steve, we will continue driving to Toronto, even if what they tell us is the worst news imaginable. If Steve has died, my dad will not be able to drive the rest of the way back, and I am worried about him and his ability to cope.

Even now, in these most trying of circumstances, I am still the eternal caregiver. In fact, at times Steve has referred to me as "Flo," a nod towards the nurse Florence Nightingale. I have learned that this is not always such a good trait to have; eventually, even Florence Nightingale burns out.

Ten minutes later, my cell phone rings.

"This is Constable Adam L. Is this Danielle?" His voice is extremely soft; the phone is full of static. I try to respond but he doesn't seem to hear me. He continues to speak. "I'm on a satellite phone and it's difficult to hear. We are in a remote location."

Normally I'm soft-spoken. This time I yell. "IT'S DANIELLE. I CAN HEAR YOU!" We are struggling to communicate. This goes on for thirty nerve-wracking seconds. Eventually I shout, "I CAN HEAR YOU, JUST TELL ME ABOUT STEVE!"

"I am with your husband Stephen." His voice remains calm. "He is severely injured. He has hurt his back and can't really move." Then a pause. "He wants to talk to you."

My first thought: *He's alive!* Then an overwhelming fear takes over; the words "hurt his back" and "can't move" run through my head. I understand the severity of spinal injuries from my years working in hospitals.

The next sound is Steve's voice, trembling. "Dans, can you hear me?"

He sounds incredibly weak, but he's talking. My voice trembles, "Steve are you okay? How is your spine?"

"Dans, my back really hurts, hard to move."

"Can you move anything? Can you feel your hands and feet?"

The clinician in me resurfaces. My years of experience take over. I will come to rely on my medical experience and clinical approach many times over the next few years, a tactic which will help me cope.

"Yes, I can wiggle my fingers and feet."

Good news. But his weak voice sounds so different than the strong Steve I know. The satellite phone is not helping as it fades in and out. Now it's barely a whisper. "Dans, I am coming home in one piece, like I promised you! I will be okay. I will be home in one piece. I promise you."

He has remembered the exact words he said to me more than two weeks before on our driveway. The threat that I made to him that day now haunts me. Somehow, I remain calm. I tell him to hang in there and that we will get through this, as we always do. "I love you!" I shout into the phone.

Constable Adam L comes back on the phone and tells me that a truck driver named Frank was the first to find Steve, who had been lying on the side of the road. They now have him on a flat board and are moving him into an ambulance, en route to Ross River, a town about two hours away. There is a small medical clinic there, and they will radio ahead to the nurse on duty to prepare.

My mother has been sitting still the entire time. Finally she speaks, saying all that matters is that he's alive. "We can deal with the rest," she assures me.

All I can think is, "F--k, Steve has a spinal injury; this is not good."

There is so much to process, and so much remains ahead. I call Michael to fill him in. Relieved that Steve is alive, he begins tracking Steve's journey to Ross River. He searches for the phone number of the remote Yukon clinic so that we can contact someone there. Thank goodness for Google.

My dad is still behind us, completely unaware of Steve's condition. Now that we know Steve is alive, we pull into the next gas station to tell him. While my mom and I cope well in crisis, my dad is sensitive and cannot contain his emotions. As I describe the phone call with the officer and Steve, my dad grows pale. Tears begin to trickle down his face.

I'm so concerned about my dad driving alone that I insist my mom get in the car with him. I just want them to get home safely and sleep in their beds. They are exhausted and stressed and this is only the beginning.

For the next forty minutes, I drive home alone, trying to hold it together. Michael texts with the phone number to the Ross River Health Centre. I ask the receptionist to call me as soon as the ambulance arrives. The remainder of the drive is a blur, but I do remember getting regular calls from the two operators at the Satellite Emergency Center in Texas. They keep me informed the whole way.

All the way home, my mind hums. How am I going to work out what to do? My family is all over the place. I'm headed to Toronto, Steve is injured in Yukon, and Josh and Gabi are in Parry Sound at Camp Manitou, three hours north of Toronto.

It's midnight when I finally arrive home. My stomach is in knots and my throat is tight. I'm terrified of what lies ahead. The first thing I do is look up the Health Centre to get as much information as possible. My heart sinks when I realize that it's a tiny facility with only a community nurse practitioner on call.

After taking my mom home, my dad comes over to stay the night. He doesn't want me to be alone (this is the "Papa Bear" in him). We track Steve's progress. It seems to take forever, but finally the ambulance arrives in Ross River. At around three am I speak to the nurse on call. She says that Steve is in good spirits. His vital signs are good, but she is concerned about his spine. She tells me that the middle part of his back is very swollen; it could be a significant injury. He is still lying flat on the ambulance stretcher.

The nurse calls the hospital in Whitehorse to discuss Steve's medical status. They decide to take him via ambulance to Faro, a small town about seventy kilometres northwest of Ross River. A small, medically equipped Cessna plane will land there and transport him to the hospital. Whitehorse General Hospital is a fifty-five-bed, full-service hospital with emergency care and advanced diagnostic imaging. The emergency team will assess Steve and decide what to do next.

For the next few hours, I wait for Steve to be transferred to Whitehorse. I lie down on my bed in our silent house. I can't sleep—how can I, with so many thoughts running through my head? I tell myself something Steve would always say: "Don't worry about things you have no control over." But I'm not yet ready to heed this advice. I don't sleep all night and won't have a good night's sleep for an exceptionally long time.

Fairly early in the morning, I call Steve's sister Maxine to let her know about the accident. Shocked, she comes right over. By now, Steve has arrived at Whitehorse General Hospital. I call the emergency department and speak with the nurse. Steve is being assessed by the ER doctor. The nurse says the radiologist or physician will call me once they have the results from the CT scan.

Waiting for the call is brutal. For nearly two decades of working in hospitals, I know all about spinal injuries, and I've seen the damage first-hand. The only difference now is that my husband is the patient. This is my worst nightmare come to life.

It is now early morning July 17. The radiologist calls. Despite no sleep, I'm still thinking clearly as he speaks. "Mrs Kaplan, your husband is alert and talking but in a lot of pain. He injured his spine in the accident. We are deciding where to send him from here because he will require surgery."

Explaining that I've worked in spinal units, I ask the doctor to tell me exactly what the X-ray shows.

"Stephen has a burst fracture of T6, with some fragments extending into the spinal canal. He'll need surgery to stabilize his spine. I have sent his CT scan results to hospitals in Calgary and Vancouver, so that he can have spinal surgery as soon as possible."

I ask the doctor if there is any way Steve can be airlifted back to Toronto. Maybe we can get him into Sunnybrook or Toronto Western hospitals where they have trauma and spinal units. I have contacts at both and know excellent surgeons. But the doctor says Steve's spine is too unstable to make such a long trip home and should be airlifted to the closest spinal unit as soon as possible. He promises me they're doing everything they can and that he will call me back shortly.

Now I have so many calls to make, to my mom, our extended family, my friends, Steve's colleagues. And of course, I need to call the kids at camp. Where do I start?

The radiologist calls back to say that Steve has been accepted at Vancouver General Hospital (VGH) and will be airlifted there that morn-ing. This is devastating for me, as Vancouver's medical system is unfamiliar to me and it's so far from home. Little do I know that we will be eternally grateful for the decision to go to VGH. It may be the single most important decision that determines Steve's fate.

I need to get to Vancouver today, to the hospital, to be with Steve. Maxine books us a flight to arrive in Vancouver at four. Friends of hers who live in the city will pick us up from the airport. They have already booked us into a hotel near the hospital. Plans are coming together quickly. It's early

Sunday morning and my house is full of so many people who care about us, all trying to arrange what needs to be done. Everyone is so supportive. They just want to be here for me, for us.

I need to call the camp where Josh and Gabi are working to tell the kids about their father. How am I going to tell them? What should I say? I need to choose my words carefully and keep my voice calm, keep things simple and optimistic. I don't want this to impact their summer. How typical of a mother always trying to protect her children. Yet how could this news not impact them?

Strangely, before Steve left on his trip, I'd worried that should anything happen to him, Josh and Gabi's experience at the camp they love would be ruined. It was a pessimistic thought, but it was so important for me that my kids have a great summer.

Steve always tells me that I worry too much about the future and that I focus on unknown possibilities and create unnecessary anxiety. This has always irritated him, as he prefers to live in the moment. He thinks about things he can control and deals with them as they happen. I am the opposite; I anticipate the worst and worry about what may happen, which often proves to be a waste of time and energy. Amidst the fear, anxiety, and practicalities of the moment, inside a small part of my head, I'm mad at Steve for creating this situation. But I bury this feeling for a very long time—and focus for now on the events that happen next.

Mark, one of the directors of Camp Manitou, is a friend, and I explain what has happened to Steve. We discuss a plan: he will find Josh and Gabi and bring them to his office in an hour, so I can call them and tell them about their dad. What will they think? How will they react? It's highly unusual for them to be taken from their responsibilities and brought into the office together. And it will certainly be unnerving for them to sit there and wait for my call. We decide that Mark will tell them that Steve has been in an accident, but that he is okay, before I speak with them to have my call be less of a shock and a surprise.

I dread telling my children about their father. My adrenaline surges but I steel myself and prepare what to say. I need to stay reassuringly calm and be factual. Again, the thought hits me that my family is split across the country while we're in a crisis. I need to be there for everyone and it's impossible. I can't be in three places at once.

There is so much to manage before the phone call with my children—cancel the Pilates classes I teach, board our dog Maddy, close the house, pack for Vancouver, and I have only three hours before I leave for the airport. My family and friends help as much they can, but it's still overwhelming.

Mark texts to let me know that my kids are in the camp office. My heart races so fast and I'm convinced they'll hear it through the phone. I go into a quieter room, away from the noise and the people, to be able to focus and do the best I can under the circumstances.

At this point, I decide that I simply must cope, be optimistic, and manage like I always do. I cannot fall apart and need to hold it together for my family. I will be the person they need me to be. They have always been the most important in my life and I never want to let them down.

I force a positive vision in my mind—Steve a week before he left for his trip. We had taken the kids to the buses to leave for camp. I remember looking at my husband and feeling proud of him. He looked great. He was strong, having worked hard to get into shape for his trip, which now, looking back, I realize is one of the factors that saved him. I felt so proud of my family that day at the bus. All was good, and I had this fit, smart, attractive man whom I loved going on an exciting adventure. My kids were healthy and having adventures of their own. I brace myself, take a deep breath, and use all my resources to make the call. Somehow, in the calmest voice I can muster, I explain what's happened.

"Hi guys! I know that you must be concerned about why I'm calling." I explain, "Dad had an accident on the bike. He's hurt his back and is going to need surgery. I've spoken to him a few times and he is good. I'm flying out to Vancouver with Maxine to be with dad. I know that he'll be fine. You know dad. He's strong and will bounce back from this. He always does!"

The kids are noticeably quiet, listening to every word. Josh and Gabi typically don't like to verbalize their feelings or ask too many questions. They are both shocked, despite me keeping things as light and positive as possible.

For years, our family has had our own inside joke about my trepidations towards Steve's motorcycle adventures. So they both ask, "Are you going to kill him?"

"For sure!" I reply. "I'm going to kill him, when I see him, for all of us."

We laugh nervously and talk about camp for a few minutes. I try to downplay the situation. I tell them I'll call them again when I see Steve. I tell them to try and get on with their days at camp, to keep busy, to have fun, and not to worry. They have incredible support; their closest friends are with them; they are in a safe, comfortable environment.

I know it won't be easy for them, but I trust that they will manage, somehow. I need to believe that—we all do. It does not cross my mind to suggest that Josh and Gabi leave camp to meet me and Steve in Vancouver. I do not want to disrupt their camp experience. At this initial moment, they do not raise the question and instead wait for me to provide further information.

* * *

Maxine and I catch the afternoon flight to Vancouver. Although I have no idea what I'm taking with me, my bags are packed and we're on our way to the airport. Waiting in the airport terminal is hard. I try to eat, but I'm not hungry. We're flying to an unfamiliar hospital in a distant province, where my husband is in an unknown condition. This is what I always feared: everything in my life has suddenly changed.

After we board the plane, Steve calls me from his cell phone. He says he's in the emergency ward at VGH waiting to be seen by the trauma team. He tells me he's okay, but in pain and lying flat on his bed, not able to move or turn. He says that he has been on two medivac flights. He sounds somewhat like the strong, practical person I know, although his voice is softer and strained. I can hear the pain seep through his voice.

He doesn't fully comprehend the implications of his situation. His spine is broken and yet he doesn't have a full sense of what lies ahead. Unsure what else to do, I tell him we will be there soon and that we will get through this together.

I manage to sleep a bit on the plane. When I'm awake, I look out the window, tears streaming silently down my face. When we land in Vancouver, I feel so displaced, so disconnected. People are hugging, smiling, talking on their cell phones. I want to be with Steve so badly, but at the same time I want to run away, back home, where things are safe and predictable.

Maxine's friends pick us up from the airport and drive us in their car to the hotel. They are all talking. I see their mouths moving, but I don't process what they're saying. The whole experience feels surreal. It's Sunday afternoon. The day before, I was basking in the sun on the boathouse deck. Now I'm being driven in someone's car, in a different city, approaching one of my greatest fears—my husband, injured from an accident on a trip he didn't need to take. A risk he didn't need to experience. One moment that's changed our lives forever.

We check into the Holiday Inn on Broadway, the closest hotel to the hospital. I have no idea how long I will be here. We leave our luggage and hurry over to the hospital. When we arrive, we are directed to the spinal step-down unit (the spinal ICU) on the ninth floor. Little do I know that I will walk these steps and ride these elevators hundreds of times over the next five weeks.

We follow the signs to the nursing station. Having worked in a hospital for so many years, everything looks so familiar and yet so foreign. A nurse tells us where to find Steve. He's in a room, enclosed by glass walls, with the curtains drawn. It is quiet. I haven't seen my husband in almost three weeks, and this isn't how I pictured our reunion. I know hospital protocol all too well, so I check with the nurses first to see if we can go in. My intimate knowledge of how hospitals work, and my past working experience, will prove invaluable throughout Steve's entire illness.

As we open the door, I don't know what to expect. But when I see Steve lying immobile on his hospital bed, hooked up to an IV and a catheter, the first thing that strikes me is that his face is so tanned. He looks strained and tired perhaps, but without any facial injuries. It's so reassuring to see Steve look like himself. I'm not sure what I expected. But I do notice that the evil eye bracelet is nowhere in sight, probably lost on the gravel road.

I kiss him and take his hand. Questions spill out of me. "Are you in pain? Can you move? What happened? What did the doctors say? What is the plan?"

I don't say what I've really been thinking. "You crazy, free-spirited, irresponsible boy! Why did you let this happen? How could you be in this situation? I told you when you left not to get injured!"

I promise myself that this is the last time I will let these thoughts enter my mind. What is the point? What is done is done and the reasons, the circumstances, no longer matter. There is no point in wondering what could and should have been. We can only deal with what is happening now. The only thing we have control over is the present. At times in our journey my anxiety will get the better of me, but I always try to focus on the present, a constructive choice for me.

Looking back, it's this new mindset that enabled me not to fall apart. In fact, this decision changes how I try to look at most things in life. I don't dwell on what was or what might be; I don't rehash what has happened or try to anticipate the future. I know that if I did it would just lead to more anxiety.

Ironically, this is how Steve has always lived his life. For years, he's been trying to convince me of his perspective. Now, I get it, even though it's taken a crisis to realize it. This may have been a preventable accident, but it's too late to dwell on that. Life is full of unpredictable events, and I must cope the best I can.

Whenever my kids face adversity, I advise them to think of the big picture and to find something positive to focus on. I've always told them that we will get through things somehow. It's finally time to follow my own advice. If only things were that simple.

Shortly before the accident, I attended a motivational talk by an exercise physiologist who made some statements that resonated with me: *Be your best when your best is needed* and *Never be derailed; stay on track*. Remembering these concepts helps anchor me, giving me a sense of control at a time when I am sinking. It isn't until much later that the impact of this trauma will hit me head on, making me feel angry, sad, and cheated.

Back in the hospital room, Steve's in terrible pain. The slightest movement is unbearable. The trauma team in the emergency ward has assessed him, and all he knows is that he needs to have spinal surgery. His wonderful nurse fills us in on his condition. She says his vital signs are stable, and they are waiting for the spinal surgeon to evaluate him and schedule the surgery.

The whole time, Steve never releases my hand. He even manages to crack a weak smile. It's obvious how relieved he is that Maxine and I are here. I reassure him that we will stay with him as long as is necessary. I tell him that I spoke with Josh and Gabi and that they seem to be coping well. I try to stay lighthearted, remarking that I'm thankful he didn't ride into the kids' camp on visitors' day like a crazed adventurer and embarrass Gabi in front of her friends. We laugh together, and I feel a faint sense of normalcy.

We have so much to catch up on. I tell Steve about the past twenty-four hours and how his sister Maxine has been a pillar of strength, logical and organized. She hasn't wavered for one second through this entire ordeal. You learn who you can depend on when a crisis arises—who walks the walk and whom just talks, who measures up and who steps back.

After about an hour, a young doctor walks into the room and introduces himself. Dr. Robert L is the orthopaedic surgeon who will operate on Steve's spine. His approach is kind, gentle, and informative. Immediately, I feel at ease and confident in his abilities, intuitively liking and respecting this man.

I don't know this at the time, but for months after this first visit, I will depend on Dr. L as both a surgeon and friend. He is committed, caring, and involved beyond what is expected. He is always concerned with how I am coping. This busy surgeon makes himself available, whether to discuss medical problems or simply to talk. He is always so encouraging, assuring me of the valuable role I play in Steve's recovery.

Dr. L explains that Steve has a burst T6 (thoracic vertebra 6) fracture and T5 spinous process fracture. He requires surgery to stabilize his spine and the fusion will likely be extensive—from T3 to T11, almost his whole thoracic spine. But there is also good news. Dr. L tells us that Steve is incredibly lucky, as he has no neurological impairments or paralysis. There is a bony fragment near the spinal canal which could have easily damaged his spinal cord. He is fortunate as this loose bony fragment did not impinge on the cord during the initial fall or during Steve's unsafe transfer into the trucker's transport rig.

Dr. L explains that Steve is essentially stable, and they are trying to determine when they can get him into the operating room (OR). Unfortunately, he tells me this will most likely not be until the following day. Believe it or not, there are patients more critical than Steve, each facing their own mortality, each with their own story to tell. There are five motorcycle accident admissions with spinal injuries this week alone. Some are in worse condition than Steve.

We will eventually get to know some of these patients and their families. We will swap details of how the injuries occurred, describe medical complications, celebrate early progress, or, in some cases, empathize over pain and deterioration. We will share pizza and stories, bonding over crises and intertwined fates. But, for now, Maxine and I decide it is time to contact our families who have been anxiously a waiting news on Steve's condition. We call our family in Toronto; Steve's sister Beulah in South Africa; and my brother, Paul, a critical care physician living in Norfolk, Virginia.

I also call the camp so that they can update my children. I take a picture of Steve giving an "I'm okay" thumbs-up sign that I send to the kids. When I reach Josh and Gabi, I tell them that their dad is doing well and promise to keep them informed. They want to know if they should come to Vancouver, but I advise them that at this point it is not necessary; they should just wait and see what happens.

Although we are both exhausted and somewhat in shock, Maxine and I make plans to get all of Steve's riding gear and clothing delivered home. His personal belongings are in bags on the hospital room floor. It occurs to me that someone must have collected his belongings off the roadside and sent them along with him to Vancouver.

I later discover just how amazing and caring the RCMP officers were when they first met up with Steve and Frank, the truck driver. Constable Adam L took the time to scour the road and bushes at the accident site and send us everything he could find.

I get in touch with Steve's colleagues from Brita, the water filter company where Steve handles the finances and operations. We'll send all Steve's work belongings to Toronto to be kept at his office until we get home. If all goes well after surgery, we plan to be in Vancouver for a week or two and then fly back home for his recovery and rehabilitation.

Steve is hooked up to a catheter to urinate and an IV for hydration and pain medication. He is not allowed to drink or eat while awaiting surgery. Although we are in an unfamiliar situation, it feels natural for me to be in a hospital. My previous work experience clicks in, enabling me to ease into my clinical persona. To help manage Steve's care, I begin to regard him as a patient, something that, over the next few years, he quietly resents.

* * *

Despite everything, Steve is coping quite well. He's already asked one of the nurses for his iPad so he can check his work emails. This is so typical of my workaholic husband, always focused and never wanting to fall behind. So what if he just suffered a severe spinal injury, was flown in two medivacs, is in pain and has barely slept? This won't deter him from catching up with work.

He says that just before we arrived at the hospital, he wrote an email to update his friends, family, and colleagues who have been following his trip website. Before leaving Toronto, Steve nicknamed his trip "Alaska or Bust," which he also uses as the subject line of his email. I think he copied the name from the lyrics of a song. The irony is almost too much. Was this a title or a premonition?

CHAPTER 3

SUBJECT: Alaska or bust . . .
DATE: July 17, 2011 6:54:12 PM PDT
FROM: Stephen Kaplan

"I GUESS THE SUBJECT of this year's Alaska trip was too prophetic . . . yesterday evening I had a bust and crashed my bike while riding the seldom travelled Campbell Highway (The 540 km sand road between Carmacks and Watson Lake in the Yukon—Like going from Toronto to Montreal, standing on the foot pegs and maybe seeing one or two other travelers along the way). It was raining and I hit a massive pothole and lost control of the bike. Fortunately, the bike slid away from me, flew into the bushes and I landed on my back sliding along the gravel road. I think I did a roll or two, but can't really remember (although I was wearing my heavy-duty riding gear, had it have been asphalt, I would have been worse off).

Anyway, when I finally realized what had happened and was laying on the floor my back hurt like mad. I did the usual self-examination checks to see if I could move my toes and fingers and all was ok, but I couldn't move without major pain. Thankfully my SPOT locator had broken away from the bike and was lying three feet away from me. I pressed the 911 button and prayed that the SPOT worked as advertised. (The SPOT office in Texas would contact the closest emergency services as well as Danielle, who was a named contact, without knowing what had happened to me, but knowing that the user was in some kind of trouble.)

Now for those of you who camp or cottage and know from mosquitoes, the Ontarian ones are babies compared to the giants in the Yukon and I was an enticing meal. Someone was looking over me, because the bag at the back of my bike was ripped apart and my unused mosquito net and bug spray was lying on the ground. I dragged myself to the lifesavers and covered my face and hands. Next was time to be concerned that the SPOT actually worked, so I pressed the 911 button a number of times. Nothing was happening for an hour and half, and I became concerned I would be bear bait, as it was getting darker, with no one around and me being unable to move. Eventually a truck came by and stopped when he saw me lying on the side of the road. I always wanted to see what the trucker's life was like, but not under these circumstances. Somehow, we got me in the truck and I lay down in the cab behind the driver and off we went to Ross River (Yukon), the closest community in the area. After about 15 minutes of driving the RCMP and an ambulance arrived. The SPOT had worked . . .

So off to Ross River, where they have a nursing station, for some preliminary checks from a registered nurse. Then back in the ambulance to Faro (Yukon) to be airlifted to Whitehorse (Yukon) for X-rays and a cat-scan. Preliminary results were fractured vertebrae 6, 7 & 8. The hospital in Whitehorse didn't have the facilities to do any spinal work, so the next step was to be airlifted to Vancouver (BC) for further investigation. So, the end result is that tomorrow morning (Monday) I have to have a metal brace inserted to help mend my spine.

Danielle and Maxine have just arrived in Vancouver and are on their way to the hospital. I don't know how long I'll be here, but it looks like I'm in good hands. Everyone involved, from the trucker, the RCMP, the three sets of paramedics and finally the Vancouver hospital staff have all been great.

I missed getting a photo because I couldn't reach my camera, but maybe it's for the better . . ."

Back in Steve's hospital room, I'm unaware how significant this email is. For months, he will have little memory of writing it nor of the events following the accident. Without this email, we would never have learned the circumstances of the accident from Steve's firsthand perspective. Even today, his memory is limited to the bike crash and the beginning of his journey to Ross River. After that, his understanding of his unlikely tale of survival comes primarily from what he has been told.

Steve's email doesn't capture the magnitude, the absolute "miracle," of what has happened to him or of how blessed he is. I don't often use the word "blessed" or even believe in miracles, but I can't think of another way to express what has happened. I've pieced together the story of the accident using input from Steve, the RCMP and photos taken at the time, and I do my best to summarize the events here.

The old Campbell Highway in Yukon stretches 583 kilometres from Carmacks to Watson Lake. It is not much of a highway. It's more of a gravel road full of potholes, known to be rough and slippery. On July 16, sixteen days into his trip, Steve is riding on the narrow stretch between the turnoff for Ross River and Watson Lake. There is little traffic; he has gone hours without seeing a soul.

According to Steve, he's travelling at a moderate speed. (I know only too well that my definition of "moderate" is a lot different than his.) He could have taken the well-travelled and paved Alaska Highway, but his adventurous nature has led him straight onto the gravel road, in the rain, just before dusk falls.

The road is wet and muddy. He drives through, rather than around some of the smaller potholes to avoid sliding. He's aware of a large pothole ahead of him but doesn't realize how deep it is as it's filled with rainwater. He decides to ride through it, standing up on the pegs of his motorcycle to take the impact on his legs. But when his front wheel gets caught in the pothole, the bike suddenly decelerates and flies up in the air, without Steve, before crashing into the bush, breaking trees, and landing on its side about twenty metres away.

Steve, too, is sent soaring until he hits the ground, hard. He lands on the right side of his body, as evidenced by the bruising to his midsection and the damage caused to his heart. The pain in his back is intense. He can't move. Although he doesn't realize it yet, his spine is broken. He remains conscious and remarkably lucid as he lies on the road wondering what to do next.

What follows is the first of what I can only describe as a series of miracles, the many inexplicable events, strokes of luck, and sheer fate that help Steve defy the unlikeliest of odds.

On all his previous trips, Steve kept his SPOT locator in his backpack. For some reason, this time he attached the device to the front of his motorcycle on a metal bracket. In retrospect, this wasn't such a good idea. We have since been told the SPOT locator should always be attached to the body of the user.

As Steve lies injured on the road, he can't see his motorcycle. He has no idea how damaged it is or where it has fallen. The SPOT locator, meanwhile, has landed just out of his reach. He spots it lying a foot or so away and struggles to shift his body towards the device. He presses the emergency button, hopeful.

The odds of what has happened are almost nil, the circumstance almost too incredible to believe. Somehow, the bright orange SPOT locator has broken off from the metal bracket quite a distance from Steve, likely by the force of the motorcycle and ground colliding. The bike is now well out of sight in the bushy terrain. The dislodged SPOT locator somehow flies up in the air about fifteen to twenty metres and miraculously lands next to him. What is the chance of that phenomenon happening? If you think about it, the SPOT (his lifeline) could have landed away from Steve in *any direction, any position, or any distance* from him, who is essentially immobile. It is like Steve is the target and the SPOT is drawn to him. What are the odds of the device landing within his reach? Talk about luck on his side! The implausibility of that is like winning the lottery of life? If the SPOT did not land within his reach, the outcome may have been quite different. The emergency response team would not have been notified so efficiently or at all, I would not have been contacted, the Emergency medical services (EMS) and RCMP would not have been alerted, and Steve's acute medical issues would have been up to Frank alone to navigate. Steve has always had good karma in life, but this is good fortune, luck, fate, and chance magnified beyond ones' imagination. This unbelievable fortuity still astounds me.

Steve knows his location is extremely remote. He fears that even though he has pressed the emergency button several times, the signal might not be picked up. He has not seen a car or truck for hours. He worries he is out of signal range. He is unaware that the SPOT system has worked, transmitting the emergency signal to the response team in Texas.

Stuck, barely able to move or even pull himself up, Steve lies on the ground in terrible pain. He worries that he's at the mercy of the elements—the insects and animals that surround him in the wild. His belongings are strewn all over the road and in the bushes. But his sleeping bag and a bottle of Advil are within reach. He takes two pills to try and dull the pain and places the sleeping bag under his head.

Then he finds his most treasured items of all—bug spray and a mesh bug net. In all his travels, Steve has never used insect repellent or a net, though he's always brought it as part of his kit. But now he's being bitten alive by huge mosquitoes that swarm all over him. When he sprays the repellent on his rain-soaked face, it runs into his eyes and burns them. Thus, he puts the bug net over his face. The rest of his belongings—clothes, cell phone, computer, snacks, camera, and wallet—are still on the bike, on the road, or in the bush. But at least he can ward off the bugs.

Steve knows that in this remote area of the bush, he's in real danger. Even though he has survived the accident, he has no idea whether someone will find him or even if he will make it through the night. He can hear animal sounds nearby. He is aware that this is grizzly bear country; there's a chance that if he stays here, he could be mauled. Perhaps, for the first time in his life, he feels helpless, out of control and frightened. He tries to work out survival strategies, but there's nothing he can do except think and wait.

He hears a helicopter flying somewhere above him and wonders if they can see him. Are they, by some chance, looking for him? Did the SPOT system work? His hopes rise. Then the sound grows faint and disappears, along with his optimism. The helicopter either is not looking for him or has missed him. Steve is left alone with his thoughts and fears.

An hour and a half passed before he hears the noise of a vehicle. A large truck is approaching. He waves his arms to flag down the driver and feels an overwhelming sense of relief. The transport truck driver stops and climbs down from his large rig, Frank. I think of him as another miracle, the second that has come Steve's way.

Frank is returning home after a few days on the road. The Campbell Highway is a shortcut to his house in Faro. It is only by chance that he is driving on this stretch of road so late in the day. At the last minute, he decided to visit a friend in Watson Lake, not something Frank would usually do, delaying his drive home. Otherwise, he and Steve would have crossed paths on an earlier stretch of the highway before Steve's accident. Chance and timing have brought Frank and Steve together.

Frank can see Steve is badly hurt. Although he understands it's probably not a good idea to move him, Frank is concerned about grizzlies, especially at dusk. It's not safe to be out there, and he suggests they get Steve into the truck as soon as possible. My husband is unable to move due to the immense pain. He knows that with an injured back, he should wait until medical help arrives prior to being moved. He tells Frank to call for assistance or to drive and get help.

Frank says that he can't leave Steve on the roadside; the chances of getting eaten by a bear are in his estimation too high. There is no cellular access and Frank's CB radio range does not extend far enough. They both hear animal noises in the bush. They decide that it's risky for Steve to be moved but riskier for him not to be. They feel they have no choice but to get Steve into the truck—it may exacerbate his injury, but it could also save his life.

Moving Steve into the rig is an overwhelming task. He's in excruciating pain, which is aggravated by any movement. Frank's truck is large, with a door a few feet off the ground. To get Steve inside involves crawling, pulling, pushing, dragging, lifting, and using their joint strength, until Steve can reach the pull bar to help Frank lift him into the door of the rig.

Steve recalls using all his upper body strength to try and get his body upright enough to pull with his arms, while Frank lifts from below. Fortunately, Frank is a big and strong man. Steve isn't a large guy, but at this point it's like lifting over 70 kilos of dead weight. He recalls being in the most intense pain of his life, nothing like he has ever experienced before. He's bent over and unable to straighten his back. Only adrenaline, fear, and urgency enable them to get Steve into the passenger seat, but the pain in a sitting position is too overbearing and so Frank rolls Steve into the bunkie bed behind the front seats.

Once again, Steve is unbelievably lucky. By moving from the road to the rig, and again from the front seat to the bunkie, his spine could have been damaged beyond repair. Although he doesn't know it yet, he has broken multiple vertebrae in his thoracic spine and has loose bony fragments in the space between the vertebrae and the spinal cord. These fragments could have pushed into his spinal cord, severing it and resulting in paralysis. In fact, the impact of the accident alone could have easily resulted in paralysis (or even death).

Though Steve has been the beneficiary of much fortune, the excruciating pain in his back makes him feel otherwise. Frank starts driving towards the Community Health Centre in Ross River. Fifteen minutes later, good fortune strikes again: the RCMP and an ambulance are driving towards them. After assessing Steve's vital signs and injuries, the paramedics transfer him onto a spinal board and load him into the ambulance. It's at this time that Constable Adam L calls me on his satellite phone. Steve is lucid and wants the police officer to let me know that he is injured but alive.

The rest of Steve's journey—the ambulance to Ross River, the two medivac planes to Whitehorse and then Vancouver—remain somewhat vague in his memory. He recalls talking to a nurse and speaking to me on the phone, but mostly he remembers the pain.

Steve's account is spotty and biased by the imprecise nature of human memory and the unrelenting pain and trauma from his accident. To learn more about the nature of his crash, I read through the RCMP Occurrence Details Report. I include key excerpts below:

18:36 pm Cst L off duty advised by telecom's that a SPOT 911 call had just been received from the Ross River Detachment area. Telecom's went on to advise that the 911 activation centre from Texas had called and advised that a lone 54 year old male (Stephen KAPLAN) had been on his motorcycle in the Yukon travelling from Alaska to Ontario. Telecom's also advised Kaplan was 5'9", Caucasian wearing Khaki pants, black and grey jacket and driving a yellow and grey BMW motorcycle. Telecom's advised Cst L they would send the GPS coordinates received in an email.

Approx 18:45 pm Cst L and Cst N attended the detachment and were given coordinates of Lat 61 37 27.2n and long 130 22 13.6w. Telecom contacted Cst L advising that they ran the co-ordinates and it appeared the signal had come from the Southwest Finlayson Lake region towards Watson Lake on the Robert Campbell Highway. Telecom's also confirmed at this time that contact had been made by SPOT representatives to the registered owners. Telecom's provided Cst L with a contact number for KAPLAN of 416 (redacted) at this time.

Cst L and N then gathered survival gear/equipment and headed towards the scene. Before exiting town, members advised local nurse/EMS of the situation and requested she have EMS staff head in the direction of the accident until stood down. It was advised that she would get the ambulance attendants moving.

Telecom advised at this time that a second and third hit/signal had been received from the SPOT device. Members advised telecom's to contact Ross River EMS to confirm they would get an ambulance headed in the direction of the possible accident.

Approx 20:30 pm at km 220 of the Robert Campbell Highway members were met by an oncoming transport truck. The male involved in the accident, Stephen Kaplan, was inside the truck lying down on the bunk. Cst N entered the vehicle and spoke with Kaplan. Kaplan advised he was experiencing pain in the centre region of his back but was able to feel all his extremities. Cst L advised telecom that they would remain on the scene until EMS volunteers attended.

Approx 20:50 pm EMS arrived on scene and telecom's advised. Kaplan placed on a backboard and taken out of the truck through the bunkhouse door. EMS advising they would transport Kaplan to the Ross River medical centre for assessment.

Cst L and N then continued 10 kms south on the highway and located Kaplan's motorcycle. Members gathered several of Kaplan's personal belongings and photographed the scene. After cleaning up the scene members headed back to Ross River.

Approx 23:40 Members attended the medical centre and Kaplan was given some of his personal effects. Medical staff then advised that they feared Kaplan's back may be broken and he would be transported to Faro for a medivac flight to Whitehorse for assessment. Members advised Kaplan that they would retrieve his bike the next day and leave it at the detachment. Kaplan thanked members for assistance and advised he would contact them at a later time.

Having spoken to Steve and the RCMP (and having read both their first-hand accounts), I've learned all I can about the nature of Steve's crash and initial rescue. Despite the tragic nature of the accident, Steve's been unbelievably lucky. He's already received two miracles—the SPOT device landing near him and the arrival of Frank—but it will take several more miracles to save him. Though it feels as if these events have lasted a lifetime, his medical journey is only just beginning.

CHAPTER 4

Two days later; the surgery

DESPITE BEING TIRED and in pain, Steve is in fairly good spirits as he lies in his hospital bed the night before his surgery. He shares his thoughts, which sends a shockwave across the room. "You know Dans, I really want to get back on my motorcycle when this is all done. You know, that saying, something like if you fall off a horse you need to get right back on. I think I should. It will be good for me."

I catch the astounded expression on Maxine's face. I, too, am dumbfounded by Steve's thoughtless comment under his circumstances.

It's a long evening waiting with Steve. The nurses come and go, checking his pain levels and making sure he is comfortable. We are still unsure of when the following day his surgery will be scheduled. Maxine and I are relieved to be with him, exhausted and still somewhat in shock. We return to our hotel at nine pm, knowing that Steve is optimistic and in good hands. We plan to stay for his surgery, brief recovery, and then return home. We feel, dare I say it, hopeful.

Since Steve's accident, I've been speaking with my brother, Paul. He's the Chief of Pulmonary and Critical Care Medicine at Eastern Virginia Medical School in Norfolk, Virginia. He is a world-renowned critical care physician who has written over four hundred peer-reviewed journal articles, fifty book chapters, four books, and delivered countless presentations worldwide. When it comes to the practice of medicine, I always rely on his expertise, which under these traumatic circumstances is extremely reassuring.

While Maxine and I walk up the hill to the hospital on the morning of Steve's surgery, I call Paul to discuss Steve's situation. Although my husband is strong and in good health, Paul reminds me to tell the medical team that Steve's father died from a pulmonary embolus, a clot in his lung, after being on bed rest following lower back surgery. Paul stresses how relevant this medical history is and how important it is to share with Steve's physicians.

When we arrive at the spinal unit, Steve is relieved to see us. He tells us that during the night he was uncomfortable, in pain, and unable to move. He's now feeling the enormity of his situation, no longer as lighthearted and spirited as the day before. He expresses to me, "Dans, I am bummed about not being able to finish my trip. I was looking forward to seeing the kids at camp as I had planned. I just want to get this over with quickly and go home."

As we wait for the surgery, we receive an email from Sandy, Frank's wife:

Hi Danielle,

I am Frank's wife Sandy and we are both so thankful your husband is going to be fine and is now in surgery. Words cannot describe the relief Frank feels now that he has spoken with you and knows that Steven is going to be fine. I called the RCMP yesterday because Frank was beside himself with worry, he is a very kind and gentle soul my husband and this has shaken him up a little. I would love the opportunity to speak with you and to have updates on Steven's progress. Frank said yesterday that when Steven said he always wanted to ride in a big truck, Frank wished he had said, well when you are better, I will take you to Inuvik on a trip. He sincerely means this and the two of them should definitely keep in touch, powers greater than us have put these two men in contact for a reason I am sure.

I am just on my way back to work and Frank wanted me to email you before he leaves today.

Sandy R.

By now, Steve's friends, colleagues and even some of his doctors have read his email describing the accident. The responses pour in; the concern and love we receive overwhelm us. Reading through the responses, it hits me how powerful Steve's firsthand account is, and so I forward Steve's email to Sandy along with my gratitude to her and her husband for their help and kind words. I refer to Frank as Steve's "guardian angel," a term I would rarely use.

Sandy replies in response to Steve's email:

> *Thanks so much for sharing this story with us, we just read it together. Frank just said well I guess this is what I was waiting for, now I can leave home. By the way we live in Faro and heard a plane late in the evening and wondered if it was Steven. Speaking of the 911 SPOT, it was in the truck and I will give it to the RCMP. Frank, having driven on these roads since the age of 15, was doubtful this would work in the middle of nowhere. Thank goodness for modern technology and truck drivers! Funny knowing Steven wanting to know what a truck driver's life is like on the road, I can proudly attest that Frank is one of the best, I of course think he is the best at his profession so as fate would have it, Steven [sic] got the nicest trucker on the road. I look forward to meeting you one day! And yes please keep us posted.*

> *Sandy*

Steve and I are touched by her correspondence and agree that one day we will return to Yukon to visit Sandy and Frank to thank him for saving Steve's life. Though we appreciate the message, the full significance of Sandy's words, and the impact Steve's accident has had on Frank, won't sink in until much later.

Our main concern today, and every day from here on out, is Steve's health. However, there are so many other things to address. I have to deal with his motorcycle—its condition, where to temporarily store it, and ultimately what to do with it. I must look into our insurance coverage and begin processing claims. I need to take care of our daily finances. I need to keep in contact with Steve's office and help them plan accordingly. It's overwhelming and our family is here to support us. They are, fittingly, our backbone.

* * *

Late in the afternoon, two days after the accident, Steve is finally wheeled into the pre-surgical room. He's anxious to get the surgery over with and to get his life back on track. We talk about the kids and how much he's looking forward to coming home. I tell him how lucky he is that, despite the burst fracture and the bony fragments, his spinal cord is still intact. I stress how grateful we should be. After all, it could have been so much worse; he could have been paralysed.

He looks at me, alarmed, and says, "Dans, I wouldn't want to live like that . . . to do that to you, Josh, and Gabi. You know me, and how I like to live. I wouldn't want to live with such a compromised quality of life. You know we spoke about what quality of life is for each of us. I never really thought we would have to consider it. You would know what to do for me if you have to. I know I am really lucky that I am not paralysed."

This is the moment when Steve finally realizes the severity of his situation and the possibility of a disastrous outcome. The trauma of the accident, the unrelenting pain, and the two days spent immobile on his back have given him time to think and left him feeling vulnerable. It's the first time I have ever seen him so shaken, so fragile.

We've discussed quality of life issues in the past, determining what decisions we would make for each other if we ever had to face the worst. Those conversations that were theoretical then are practical now. I reassure him that he will be strong, walking, running, and even riding again in time. Just before the operating room attendant wheels Steve into surgery, I kiss him on the forehead and tell him to have a good sleep. I tell him Maxine and I will be here when he's out of surgery. I squeeze his hand and tell him that I'll always be here and always love him, no matter what.

The surgery is scheduled to take about three hours. Maxine and I leave the hospital and walk down the hill to get something to eat. Neither of us is hungry, but we need something to do, something to occupy the time. Sitting and waiting in the hospital is too brutal.

Back in the intensive care spinal unit, we try to read or sleep, but mostly we just sit and wait. Steve's nurse comes to update us. He says Steve's back in recovery and will likely return to the spinal step-down unit in the next hour or so. We are relieved that the surgery is over; now we can focus on his recovery and make plans to go home.

Another two hours go by. It is nearly eleven and we're concerned and exhausted. We ask the nurse for another update. He calls down to the recovery room and is told that Steve has had some difficulty waking up from the anaesthetic and that his breathing is a little laboured. They have put him on oxygen.

The more time passes, the more anxious we become. Steve's empathetic nurse asks the staff in the recovery room if we can come down to see him. Three hours post-surgery, I am finally able to visit my husband. His face, covered with nasal prongs that provide him oxygen, looks tired. His speech is mildly slurred, and he seems a little disoriented, which means he's coming out of the anaesthetic slower than expected. I revert into my clinical mode and ask questions to determine his level of confusion: "Steve, where are you? Do you know what happened to you? Do you know why you had surgery?"

He begins to answer, then pauses mid-sentence, and looks straight at me. "You are not my therapist! Why are you asking me these stupid questions? I know who I am and what happened!"

We all have a good laugh. This is the Steve we know and love. But I'm not completely reassured; something doesn't feel right to me. I have a nagging feeling that this isn't going to be quite so simple.

The recovery room staff believe he's ready to go back to the spinal step-down unit. We walk alongside the porter. Steve lies on the stretcher still attached to his oxygen. Back in his glass room, the respiratory therapist (RT) monitors his oxygenation. He thinks Steve should stay on the nasal prongs for the night. Steve, still drowsy, is a little more coherent than earlier. The nurses set him up with patient-controlled analgesia (PCA), a self-administering system that allows him to top up his morphine levels when he is in pain. We wait for Steve to fall asleep and then return to our hotel to try and steal a few hours of rest ourselves.

Early in the morning, we return to the hospital. Steve's face is grey and strained. He says that he has been in the most unimaginable pain overnight—pain so intense that it is worse than immediately following the accident or when he was moved into the truck. The morphine has obviously worn off, and he isn't aware that he can top up the pain medication on his own. Once he understands that he can administer his own pain relief, he relaxes a bit. He's so afraid of experiencing that pain again that for the rest of the day he keeps his hand around the handle and his thumb hovering over the button.

His fear is palpable, and he doesn't want Maxine or I to leave him. This marks the beginning of Steve being completely traumatized by his experience. The RT is constantly in and out of the room, checking Steve's breathing, which is becoming even more laboured. The nasal prongs are exchanged for a facemask to give him more oxygen. Now, I am really worried.

When I call Paul, he's concerned about the possibility of blood clots (pulmonary emboli). It is exactly what he warned us about. He wants to speak to the critical care physician who is taking care of Steve.

The medical team—the critical care physician, pain specialist, and residents—happen to be at the nursing station doing their daily rounds. I explain that my brother is a critical care physician in the US and that he'd like an update about Steve from them. I'm interrupting their rounds, so I try to express myself respectfully but also with confidence. By this point, they are aware of my health care background and gentle yet assertive manner. They graciously agree to speak with Paul.

Before I hand over my cell phone, one of the doctors asks me for Paul's full name, I suppose, out of respect and to be able to refer to him as a fellow colleague. When I introduce my brother as "Dr. Paul M.," there is an immediate reaction. As the critical care physician speaks with Paul, another doctor turns to me and says, "That's your brother? He's like a rock star in the world of critical care medicine!"

They have the utmost respect for Paul and are familiar with his clinical research and reputation. It's sort of humorous for me to hear my brother (who ruthlessly teased me when we were kids) being referred to with such high regard. Now I'm even more assured that we are in vigilant and caring hands because the medical team is now also updating (and I suppose accountable to) Paul regarding Steve's condition. I am so grateful for this connection.

Paul shares Steve's family's medical history with the doctor who assures him that they will continue to monitor Steve for any signs of pulmonary embolus. He is already on blood thinners. Still, his respiratory distress is worrisome, and the cause remains unclear. It could be due to aspiration pneumonia, a pneumothorax, or the less likely chance of a pulmonary embolus.

Meanwhile, I receive a flood of emails, texts, and phone calls asking how Steve is doing post-surgery. I appreciate everyone's concern but can't respond to all the messages. I decide one of the easiest ways to communicate with family and friends all over the world is to post short, simple updates on Facebook. I am sparse and intermittent with my posts.

On July 19, 2011, I write:

Steve is really lucky following his accident and surgery. This morning, he's up and walking a little distance with the physiotherapist, using a high wheeled walker. However, he got worse through the day and now he's not as great, as he likely has pneumonia. This will delay his recovery. One day at a time.

The hours pass and Steve spends most of his time asleep. He still requires his pain medication and the facemask that provides oxygen. Maxine and I sit next to his bed chatting, snacking, and arranging to get his belongings back to Toronto.

Steve, at this point, is only sipping water. He is weak, in pain, and not interested in eating. We notice his worsening respiration. I see that the RT is becoming concerned too. By the evening, Steve's saturation levels are low (the concentration of oxygen in his blood), so he is put on bi-level positive airway pressure (BiPAP) for the night. BiPAP is a breathing apparatus that helps patients get more air into their lungs. It's a pressured facemask that takes takes time getting used to wearing. Steve is now extremely uncomfortable and quite drowsy. I am feeling anxious about his deteriorating condition. The night is rough for us all.

There is so much going on. We handle legal matters and insurance claims; we share relevant information with our friends and family; we advocate on Steve's behalf to his medical team. All the while, his medical condition deteriorates. Maxine and I are coping, but the gravity of the situation weighs on us. We are exhausted, worried, and feel as if we can't handle anymore.

Unfortunately, life has other plans.

CHAPTER 5

July 20

I T IS JULY 20, 2011, the day that proves to be the most intense and pivotal turning point in our lives.

Steve is now in respiratory failure and totally dependent on BiPAP for breathing support. The RT says that while Steve's oxygenation is stable, they're not sure whether his respiratory failure is due to pneumonia, atelectasis (lung collapse), or small pulmonary emboli (blood clots from the legs which have travelled to the lungs).

Though a CT scan has been booked, it is delayed. I advocate for an earlier time because of the urgency of the procedure, but to no avail. The medical team seem unaware as to the severity of Steve's deterioration, perhaps the only lapse of judgement on their part in his lengthy complex medical care.

While Maxine and I spend the earlier part of the morning sitting with Steve, his breathing is laboured, and he's uncomfortable, although he's getting used to the BiPAP mask. He's tired, weak, discouraged. Talking with the facemask on is uncomfortable for him, so he chooses not to speak. The RT and his nurse are concerned and spend considerable time in his room monitoring his respiratory status. They reassure us that he is stable and that the medical team will resolve his breathing problems.

Maxine and I leave the hospital for an hour at most to courier his belongings to his office in Toronto. When we return to the unit, we see the medical team dealing with an emergency near the nursing station. Our hearts drop when we realize that it is Steve, now on a stretcher, with nurses and doctors attending to him.

He is extremely drowsy. His nurse tells us that while he was on a short walk with the staff, still on his BiPAP, he had a hypotensive episode (excessively low blood pressure causing dizziness and fainting or shock). He is no longer conscious. It's fortunate that he was using his walker and that his nurse and physiotherapist were holding him, preventing him from hitting the floor.

Steve is rushed to the CT scanner, and we are directed to follow a nurse down to the radiology department where we can wait. Everything happens so fast, and Steve deteriorates quickly. The staff believe he has acute hypoxemic respiratory failure (insufficient oxygen in the blood). A CT scan will help determine the cause of his respiratory failure. Following the CT scan, he is taken to interventional radiology.

I tend to ask questions and research information as necessary. It's important for me to understand these unfamiliar terms, procedures, and why they are required. I cope well when I am well informed and knowledgeable. This helps when I need to advocate for Steve, make decisions, and become more assertive in his care. This is the practical, logical, and clinical me which surfaces when necessary. My panicked, anxious, and overwhelmed feelings and emotions are purposely suppressed, as there is no time or space to deal with them now.

I am asked to sign consent for the interventional radiologist to insert an IVC filter. This procedure places a filter in the inferior vena cava (IVC), which is a large vein carrying deoxygenated blood from the lower body to the heart. An IVC filter traps large clot fragments that may develop in the veins in the leg, a condition called deep vein thrombosis (DVT), and prevents them from travelling to the heart and lungs, where they could cause severe complications or even death. The medical team hope that it is not too late to place the IVC filters, but unfortunately for Steve it is.

Maxine and I are guided back to the OR waiting room. Maxine becomes quiet and withdrawn. I become quite chatty, a way of distracting myself from my thoughts.

I start talking to a family who, by coincidence, is from the Yukon. One of the men is interested in hearing about Steve's trip and knows the terrain where he had been riding. He says Steve is extremely lucky to have been found by the trucker, as he was in the heart of grizzly bear territory. He believes if Steve had stayed there all night, in all likelihood a grizzly would have attacked him.

Another woman's situation really hits me. She explains that her close friend died from leukemia in this very hospital last night and that today her young son-in-law, recently married, is facing complications with his leukemia and requires an OR procedure. This woman is so distraught and overwhelmed. She needs to vent and share her fears with me, a total stranger. I find myself distracted from Steve's situation and feel good supporting her, a much-needed reprieve from our circumstances.

It is now three hours since we came into the OR waiting room. We still know nothing of Steve's condition during the surgery to insert the IVC. After pacing the hallways, Maxine and I eventually page the critical care physician who has been taking care of Steve on the spinal unit. When he calls back, he explains they are still working on him, and he'll come to speak to us as soon as the procedure is complete, and once Steve is stable.

Shortly after, Dr. Robert L, Steve's spinal surgeon, comes to speak with us. He explains that the CT scan detected massive bilateral pulmonary emboli. He was taken to the interventional radiology suite for placement of the IVC filter, as well as aspiration of the embolus. Steve is being given intra-arterial tissue plasminogen activator (tPA), a treatment to breakdown the blood clots. This is often administered in the case of a heart attack, stroke, or acute massive pulmonary emboli.

However, since tPA dissolves blood clots, there is also the risk of haemorrhage with its use. Dr. L is concerned that Steve could start bleeding into his spinal operative site, which may cause damage to his spinal cord. This is the third time that his spinal cord has been at risk, and he could become paralysed.

Dr. L advises us that Steve is now being treated with the tPA and that we can see him when he's stable. After the procedure, he will be in the medical ICU, as his respiratory and heart rate will need to be closely monitored.

At this stage, I don't know if Dr. L is telling me all he knows or if he is gently preparing me for Steve's sharp deterioration. Dr. L's demeanour and facial expression reveal he too is deeply concerned. Perhaps paralysis is the least of our concerns.

Maxine and I continue to wait. What else can we do? I am no longer chatty. The adrenaline races through my body; my thoughts are all over the place. Dr. L's words have thrown me into a tailspin. We have no idea how much worse things can and will continue to get.

A nurse with a sombre expression comes into the waiting room and asks for Stephen K's family to follow her. We gather our belongings and walk down the hallway behind her. She stops, turns around, and simply says, "Your husband is in the ICU now. It's not good."

Not good? What do you mean not good? Wait! Stop! Explain what you mean. Don't walk away! I try to respond, but no sound comes out of my mouth.

We follow the nurse into the ICU. I am so lost in my own thoughts that I have no idea how Maxine is feeling. In front of me I see an ICU bed, with doctors and nurses surrounding it. As we walk in, we can feel the tension, then suddenly, the stillness, as all eyes turn to us. The doctors and nurses are surrounding the ICU bed, and I'm numb and disconnected.

I put my beautiful leather purse on the hospital floor in the middle of the hallway, the purse I treasure, something I would never normally do. But the only thing that matters right now is my husband. I walk forward to the bed, aware that the lifeless person lying on top of it is Steve. Watching the action in front of me is surreal. It's as if I'm in one of those chaotic scenes in *Grey's Anatomy*. It feels like a choreographed dance, a team of medical professionals weaving in and around each other with such grace. There must be at least ten health care professionals in the room.

The person on the bed *is* Steve, but it's hard for me to accept it. My husband was always full of life—the person on the bed is grey, ashen, rigid, lifeless. Is he dead? His beautiful green eyes are open, staring but not seeing. At some point, one of the nurses closes his eyelids, so he now looks like he's sleeping.

He's not breathing on his own. Oh my god, they're bagging him! He has a mask over his face attached to a rubber-like balloon. The nurse is manually compressing and pumping air into his lungs. I step forward towards him and take one of his lifeless, non-responsive hands. They continue to work on him, sliding around me as if I'm not even here. In a sense, I'm not. I'm scared and I'm in shock. Steve is dying. That much is clear.

Finally, I look away from Steve to find Maxine sitting in the nursing station on the phone, a glazed expression on her face, tears in her eyes. A surge of adrenaline rushes through me, like I'm freefalling, on a roller coaster I would never dare ride. I am falling at a great speed and am suddenly weightless. The world around me spins out of control. My legs are like jelly but somehow continue to hold me up. I want to run away, but I am glued to the spot. Amidst all the chaos, I am motionless.

I have no idea how much time has passed, likely only minutes. Dr. George I introduces himself to me as the critical care physician taking care of Steve. He says that Steve is in multi-organ failure, which means respiratory, cardiac, kidney, and liver failure. I wish I didn't know what this means. His organs are not functioning. Several specialists, including a cardiologist assess him. The doctor tells me that it's extremely unlikely that Steve will survive the next few hours.

In addition to suffering the massive bilateral embolism, they have now discovered that my husband's heart is damaged. Specifically, he has had a rupture to the tricuspid heart valve, which may have resulted from the procedure or, more likely, from the initial accident.

Steve has gone into cardiac arrest and his heart has stopped. The message from the doctor comes through loud and clear. Steve is going to die. I am in shock. I am in disbelief. I feel numb, dizzy, dazed, and powerless. There is no life left in Steve. The doctors are speaking to me, but I am unable to make sense of their words.

Later, when I can process the information more clearly, I realize exactly what happened that afternoon and evening. Steve had the IVC filters surgically placed and underwent pulmonary emboli aspiration. He received intra-arterial tPA to break down the extensive bilateral clots. He was transferred to the ICU where his breathing became shallow and too rapid (tachypneic) and was intubated for airway protection. Transesophageal echocardiography showed a clot in the right ventricle of his heart. An alteplase infusion used to treat pulmonary embolus resulted in some improvement. After all of this, Steve developed a slow heart rate (bradycardia). He required CPR for two minutes and was given one amp of epinephrine, two amps of bicarbonate, and one amp of calcium to successfully resuscitate him. Here's where the doctor called us into the room. Steve is being manually ventilated with a hand-held resuscitation device, through the endotracheal tube in his mouth. He is on the brink of death. I can see it in the doctors' eyes and in the lifeless eyes of my husband.

Our children need to be told. They know nothing of his deterioration. My last call to them was this morning to tell them that his surgery the night before was successful. I had planned to call them again when Steve was making progress. Clearly this is no longer feasible. They will be stunned and shocked to be told their dad is dying. How can I comfort and reassure them? How can I explain to them what has happened? What do I do while Steve is dying here in front of me and my children are thousands of kilometres away in a different time zone? I feel panicked, in complete disbelief and intense sadness for my children. All I could think of was how to protect them. Damn Steve, he promised me! This is almost too much to cope with.

Steve is unconscious. He is not breathing on his own. His heart has been severely shocked. His lungs are severely compromised. His liver and kidneys have stopped working. The situation couldn't be worse. One of the doctors tells me that Steve is as sick as one could possibly be.

"He will not survive the night."

I keep repeating that phrase over and over in my head.

Maxine calls our family and my brother Paul to tell them what's happening. While Paul speaks to Dr. George I, I stand holding Steve's hand, telling him that I am here with him. I want him to hear my voice. I stroke his face and run my hand through his hair. Maybe he cannot hear me or process anything I am saying or doing, but I need to feel as if I'm doing something, as if I'm comforting him. The nurses support and provide us with simple factual information. I look at Dr. Robert L. He has a strained, sad expression on his face.

Maxine is devastated. Despite our shock, we realize we need to make plans. We agree that I should fly home to be with Josh and Gabi and that she should wait here at the hospital, to take care of everything and fly home with Steve's body. So many times, I hear that he is unlikely to survive the night. The odds are totally stacked against him. We are preparing for the worst.

Even though I am in immense shock, I know what to discuss with Dr. I: "I think we need to let Steve go now. We need to stop bagging him. If he's as sick as you say, with real no chance of survival, then we need to let him go with dignity. This is not what he would want. What are we prolonging? Nothing is working."

As I am speaking, my thoughts are that he likely will have brain damage from the lack of oxygen or will be dependent on machines and technology to keep his organs functioning and him alive. This is not what Steve or I would want for him.

Dr. I says to give Steve a little time. He wants to discuss a possible but unlikely life-saving treatment with my brother Paul. Dr. I and Paul speak again, trying to work out what to do. In their opinion Steve is too young, too fit, and too strong to let him go without trying everything possible. Dr. I suggests we try a life-support procedure called extracorpeal membrane oxygenation (ECMO). He describes this procedure, stating that ECMO will act as Steve's external heart and lungs. It's a life-support system, providing both cardiac and respiratory support to people whose heart and lungs are so severely damaged that they can't function. ECMO doesn't heal organs; it only allows the heart and lungs time to rest. And it's the only possible way to try save his life, even though the chances are extremely slim. The doctor explains why he wants to do it, what it entails, and that this is the only medical procedure left that might help. He explains that he and Paul have discussed it and, although it only carries a very small chance of benefiting Steve, they both believe it's worth trying.

Reflecting upon these moments many years later, we understand how fortunate we were that Steve was sent to VGH. Calgary Hospital, the other option considered for spinal surgery, did not have ECMO. At the time, I do not fully grasp what ECMO is or what it involves, only that Steve has an extremely low prognosis for a good outcome.

My mind churns with many thoughts, so many questions. Will Steve survive? Was there a lack of oxygen to his brain? Will he regain organ function? Will he walk, communicate, solve problems, go back to work? Will he be independent or will he be reliant on others for the rest of his life?

He would hate to be dependent on anyone in any way. We have previously discussed this issue and were both clear on what quality of life means to each of us, and we revisited this conversation just prior to his surgery. The immediacy and gravity of the situation become even more apparent.

I don't have much time, so it's important to think clearly and purposefully. If we know for certain that his prognosis and his outcome will be positive, then I will say go ahead and put him on ECMO. But none of us can accurately predict the future. There is no crystal ball. He is far too compromised, too critical, with very little chance, if any, of survival. The Steve that I know is too smart, too physically active, and too accomplished to take such a risk. That Steve is now gone, and I can't subject what's left of him to this.

Paul believes that we must try any attempt to save him. He reinforces that Steve is young and was in good physical condition prior to the accident. By now Maxine has spoken to Steve's brother Michael and her husband Phillip who all think we must do everything to save Steve. I phone my parents and let them know about Steve's critical situation. I tell my mom that we need to let him go and that if it were Steve making this decision, he would not want to risk the potential outcome. My mom pleads with me to give Steve a chance. She keeps saying that he's Josh and Gabi's dad. For them, we need to give him every opportunity. Steve's family, Paul, my parents, and the doctors all want to take the chance and try ECMO. I keep wondering what's left to try and save?

Months later, Paul will tell me that in his honest opinion, based on Steve's medical condition, he had a "zero percent chance" of survival with or without ECMO. But at the time, he continues to encourage me to give Steve any chance available.

Dr. I explains that ECMO requires surgery to place a cannula in Steve's artery. He says that there's a significant risk with the procedure. I am told that Steve likely won't survive the surgery, the time on ECMO or coming off ECMO. Nevertheless, Dr. I and Paul feel we should carry out the procedure. The alternative is clear that Steve will die within the next few hours unless we don't.

I have seen trauma and the consequences of oxygen deprivation. I have seen people try and live with severely damaged organs, dialysis, respiratory support, ventilation, weakness, cognitive deficits, wheelchairs, feeding tubes, and more. Steve wouldn't want any of that and nor would I.

How do I make this decision on my own? I need Steve to help me. We are a team, but it's now only up to me. In my head, I'm begging for him to make the decision with me, for me. I can't do this alone. I whisper to him, "Steve, I know you better than anyone. We have spoken about this. Help me! Wake up! Tell me what you want! What should I do? You can't leave this for me to decide on my own. I need you! I'm so mad at you. You promised!"

He *is* dying. The decision now is whether he should be left to die or if we medically intervene. If he does survive, he will likely have a very poor outcome. Literally, his life is in my hands. I can't deal with the overwhelming pressure and weight of such a choice. What do I do? What is right?

Over and over, I debate with myself. I need to stay focused. I know that everyone wants to try ECMO, to take this miniscule chance and wait to see what happens. I feel deep in my gut that I should let him die as simply and peacefully as possible. I know then I'm respecting his wishes under these critical circumstances.

In my heart of hearts, I believed that I was prepared and would know just what to do when faced with a life-and-death decision. Now I know it's different when it's your life partner, someone you depend upon, the father of your children, and you actually have to decide. We made promises to one another. I can't take the chance that he won't recover or have a good quality of life. It's that simple. I need to say goodbye to Steve, to my boy, and let him die peacefully over the next few hours with the dignity he would want. This is a total nightmare.

Dr. George I and Dr. Robert L remain with us while we struggle to make this traumatic decision. Everyone continues to tell me that we should try ECMO, to take the chance, however small. For Steve to have ECMO requires my signed consent. It's a medical procedure, and as his wife, I am his substitute decision-maker since he is now incapable of advocating for himself.

I can exercise my legal right to refuse consent, even if the physicians don't agree with my decision. My brain is telling me not to sign the consent for this risky life-saving intervention, as the probable result is, at best, a severely compromised outcome. I can't do that to Steve. If he could talk to me, I know for sure that's what he would tell me to do. His voice won't stop running through my head: "Dans, let me go. I don't want to live like this, for me, and for you, and the kids!"

These are the facts. The ECMO is the machine used when all other medical options are exhausted. Patients who require ECMO have a mortality rate of 80–90%. One must be in grave condition for ECMO to be recommended at all. And for the 10–20% of people who survive the initial procedure, the long-term effects can be quite poor.

Steve would undergo another surgery to place the cannula into the blood vessel—in Steve's case, in the femoral artery in the groin. The cannula allows blood to be removed from the heart and travel through the ECMO circuit (heart-lung bypass machine) where it has oxygen added and carbon dioxide removed. The blood is then warmed and returned to the heart through a second cannula.

Dr. I and I go to a quiet room to talk this through together. He is so kind, patient, and thoughtful. He explains what the procedure entails and again why he thinks we should try it. Dr. I explains that if we put him on ECMO, there is a slight chance that after letting his heart and lungs rest, they may function on their own.

For most of the discussion I remain confident in my belief that we should let Steve go. Paul calls, and he and Dr. I try to encourage me to sign the consent. Paul asks me directly why I wouldn't want to take any available chance for Steve's survival. Nobody seems to understand our agreement, our pact, or know Steve in the way that I do. He would only want to live if we could assure him of a good quality of life. But we can't.

The pressure from everyone is wearing me down. We are running out of time to decide. It hits me that I am going to lose him. The Steve that my children and I love will be gone forever. Things will never be the same again. Our previous life is now over forever.

I decide to follow through on what Steve and I fundamentally believe in and not sign the consent for ECMO. I'm adamant that we shouldn't take the risk of this indignity to him. I know everyone will disagree with me and that they will be devastated and hold me accountable. But, still, I know in my gut that he would tell me to just let him go.

When I tell Dr. I of my decision, he sits quietly for a while, not saying a word. He doesn't give up and then calmly says if we put Steve on ECMO, we can evaluate how he's doing. If he doesn't change or show improvement in the next forty-eight hours, we will take him off ECMO and let him go without further intervention. "Then you will know, for you and your family, that you did your best for Stephen."

"It's not the same thing to withdraw life support from someone, as it is to decide not put him on it." I reply.

I'm so clear and so confused at the same time, trying to be rational, while falling apart inside, as I make the most critical decision of my life. If we don't try ECMO then our children and our families will always question me. Maybe they will never forgive me. Can I live with that? How can I tell Josh and Gabi my choice? They might say, "Mom, you should have tried to save dad; it wasn't only your decision."

Surprisingly, I change my mind. "I'll sign the consent to go ahead with ECMO, but if we see no improvement in a short period of time, I want you to promise me that I have the right to have it removed and that you'll listen to me. I need to know that."

Dr. I calmly promises he will honour my request. The fear of doing the wrong thing, of not listening to those who care for Steve, allows me to change my mind, to listen to everyone's pleas, to the silent voices of my children.

I sign the consent form against my own gut feeling and probably against Steve's wishes too. Perhaps it's Dr. I's confidence that motivates me. Perhaps it's my mother's words telling me we must give Steve a chance. Perhaps I'm worried I'll be blamed forever if I don't give Steve one last opportunity. Ultimately, our children still need their father. I'm not sure if I'm motivated primarily out of love or fear but, ultimately, I sign. It's a decision I'm forever grateful for, but at the time I feel nothing but pure panic.

Later, I'm told that it is nearly impossible for someone with massive bilateral PEs, a tricuspid heart valve rupture, and complete organ failure to survive. At one point, someone tells me the chances of survival are less than 1%. The odds are totally stacked against him.

When I walk back to Steve, I can hardly bear to look at him. I whisper that Josh, Gabi, and I will be okay, that we are proud of him, and that we all love him so much. I kiss him on his forehead, squeeze his hand, and tell him that I will always love him. I will take care of Josh and Gabi, Maddy our dog. I will manage. I tell him that I'm strong and he will be proud. I say goodbye.

Tears stream down my face, and Maxine's too, as we watch a nurse wheel Steve into surgery for the procedure. It is likely that we will never see him alive again. We stand motionless, in shock.

CHAPTER 6

Night of July 20 and day of July 21

THE DOCTORS ARE concerned for me and Maxine. They say that it will take several hours to know how Steve is doing and that we should get some rest. Someone will call with any updates or changes to Steve's condition. The nurses hover around and encourage us to go back to the hotel to try and get some sleep. Sleep? How can we sleep?

Being so far from home and our family feels so precarious. In a trance, Maxine and I walk towards the elevators. Not a word is said between us. It's now around eleven pm Vancouver time, two am in Toronto. Is it too early to phone my parents? I desperately need to hear my mom's voice.

What I really need is to know if Steve will survive the procedure. All I can think of are my children. I'm here in Vancouver, while they're thousands of kilometres away. I need to talk to them, see them, comfort them. How am I going to tell them the latest, almost unthinkable, news about their dad? How can I do this from a distance? I feel like I need to be in two places at the same time, but of course that's not possible. I feel sick to my stomach.

We arrive back at the hotel room and climb into bed. Still, hardly a word is exchanged between us. What is there to say? Maxine falls asleep from pure exhaustion. I lie awake, trying to work out what to do. I need to talk this through with my mom. I need to figure out what to say to my children. Most of all, I need to know if I made the right decision in signing the consent form. A small part of me hopes that Steve will not survive the surgery but rather die "peacefully" in his sleep. Is that cold, callous, unfeeling? I can't shake the thought of Steve surviving the surgery and having a poor quality of life, trapped in circumstances he expressly said he didn't want. Would he blame me for his outcome?

At this moment, I am more scared of him having brain and organ damage than I am of him dying. How terrible is that? I feel if he dies tonight, his fate will be out of my hands and I won't have to make any other overwhelming decisions on his behalf. We won't have to deal with the pain, resentment, and uncertainty that follows a poor outcome from a successful surgery.

Of course, whether he lives or dies, our lives have already been irrevocably changed. Who goes on such adventures while having a family to care for? Steve promised me he would be safe and that nothing would happen. I hate him for putting his life at risk, for destroying our lives as we know it, for changing the kids' lives forever, for stressing our families. I hate him for this.

I consider myself a thoughtful, compassionate, practical person who has been presented with the most difficult ethical dilemma. And so I'm angry with myself. I broke my pact. I promised him that I would let him die if there was ever any risk of a marked deterioration to his quality of life. Did I let him down? Why did I sign the consent? I had his life in my hands. I am devastated.

Why did I allow him to get on his damn motorcycle in the first place? Could I have stopped him? What would he have chosen—our marriage or his need for freedom? Will I ever get the answers to my questions? Above all, the same question repeats itself: How can we live without Steve?

Despite being exhausted, I am unable to sleep. The questions won't stop; my anxiety is relentless. I can't lie here any longer alone with my thoughts. I get up, shower, and wash my hair to try to distract myself. I go back to bed. Still, I can't sleep.

I call the ICU number the nurse gave me. A nurse says that Steve is now in the ICU and hooked up to the ECMO machine. She says that the IVC filter was removed, and he has survived the surgical procedure to insert the cannula and to connect him to the ECMO circuit. She reinforces that we need to wait and see how he does.

She suggests I get some sleep and call back in a few hours. I don't know if I'm relieved or disappointed that Steve is still alive while remaining so critically ill. I tell Maxine that he's survived the surgery and is now in the ICU. The relief is written all over her face. I realize that this is good news. Steve has survived the procedure even though the odds of him doing so were incredibly low. So why don't I feel happy?

It is six am Toronto time. I can't wait to hear my mom's voice. She always knows how to comfort me. She'll know what to do. She always does. When she answers, I cry just from the sound of her voice. I can tell my dad is on the line, listening. I fill them in on Steve's medical status. I tell them how scared and confused I am.

My mom reassures me that I have done the right thing for Josh and Gabi, for everyone. Steve still has a fighting chance. I ask her how to tell the children. Since I spoke to Josh and Gabi yesterday, Steve has significantly deteriorated. I should be with my children. I should be telling them, holding them, crying with them. My mom takes control of the situation, as she always does. She tells me that she and my dad will drive up to Camp Manitou later this morning. She will go with my friend Carolyn and my sister-in-law Susie. They will talk to Josh and Gabi and explain what has happened. They will stay with them for as long as necessary.

We decide that I will phone Mark, the camp director, to update him and work out how to deal with all of this. My mom and I talk through all the scenarios—how to update the kids if Steve dies and how to advise the children of the unlikely chance of Steve surviving. We agree she will have to follow their lead and decide in the moment what to say next. I will call the kids after my parents have shared the devastating news about Steve. I can't imagine a more difficult phone call.

I feel that I can cope a little better now that we have a plan. I have four people I can totally trust and depend on. They will make the three-hour drive to tell my children that the unimaginable has happened. I feel the tension in the car ride, the words both spoken and unspoken. I imagine the conversation with my children.

I call Paul, while Maxine calls Michael. Five days after Steve's accident, our brothers both are flying into Vancouver later today. It will be nice to have more support. For now, it's just the two of us. Maxine and I walk back to the hospital.

Outside the ICU, there's a buzzer we must press to announce who we are and to state which patient we are seeing. It is up to the nurse to decide if the timing is good for us to enter. Fortunately, the door opens, and we're told where to find Steve. He has been given the biggest room in the ICU to hold all the major equipment keeping him alive.

The ECMO machine is large and made up of several parts. Steve is mechanically ventilated, as well as on dialysis. His nurse, coincidentally named Steven, comes to greet us. He tells us that Steve requires round-the-clock one-on-one nursing. He acknowledges that it is overwhelming to look at Steve now: he is intubated through his mouth, has a large tube in his nose draining fluid, multiple IVs, a central line in his neck, a catheter, and a feeding tube and is hooked up to all the machines with tubing and wires. He is severely drugged to keep him still, so that there is no stress on his system, which will help his heart and lungs to rest and hopefully to heal.

I have already seen much of this before when working in ICUs, although I have never seen someone on ECMO. It must be such a shock for Maxine to see her brother like this. His eyes are partially closed, swollen, his eyelids not fully down, so we can see the white of his eyes and partial green of his irises. He is so bloated from the fluid retention and is essentially unrecognizable. It's hard to shake this image.

We stand looking down at him, at all the equipment and tubing going into and out of his face and body. He is non-responsive, so fragile, and unapproachable. I can't believe that this is Steve. I take his hand, stroke his forehead, shut his eyes. There is no response. I bend down and softly let him know that we are here. I tell him that I love him and that I'll stay with him.

I feel helpless. Everything is beyond my control. I hope my familiar voice will stimulate some awareness but know that it is unlikely. He doesn't look like himself. His face is so swollen, sweaty, and vulnerable, and yet he has a soft peaceful expression. I smile through my tears, as I notice there are none of the usual frown lines above his nose. It's crazy what enters your mind in such surreal circumstances.

Steven, his nurse, is extremely compassionate and knowledgeable. He explains all the equipment to us, the purpose of the tubing, Steve's vital signs, what they measure, and why. He explains that the biggest risk of ECMO is bleeding or clots. He says that while on ECMO Steve is sedated and chemically paralysed, and that he likely isn't aware of much.

They need to assess his responsiveness. To wake him, the nurses briefly hold back on the IV sedatives and ask him to squeeze a hand or open his eyes. Sometimes there's no response; other times his eyes open, with a blank stare or a look of panic. The startled look shocks me every time. I don't know what it means.

I decide to try and be with him whenever they wake him. I hold his hand and reassure him that he is going to be alright, irrespective of what I truly feel. We aren't sure if he is aware or if his responses are startle reflex reactions. It is horrifying seeing that look on his face.

Maxine and I spend the morning in Steve's ICU room watching his nurse monitor his vital signs; assess his functioning; and check the ventilator, arterial lines, IV bags, feeding tube, ECMO circuit, and much more. While the nurse has so much to do, we have little to do but wait.

We go for lunch because we need a break, not because we are hungry. We sit, stunned, staring at each other, picking at our food. I speak to my mom. We go over again what she should say to Josh and Gabi. We agree that she will be as truthful and honest as possible. My mom, the most empathic person I know, is the best person to share this devastating news with my children.

I feel that depending on the kids' reactions, they should be encouraged to stay at camp and not head home or here to Vancouver until we work out what is happening. I can't think beyond the next day or even the next hour. I know that I want to talk to Josh and Gabi once my parents arrive, to comfort them, and hear their voices, even if from a distance.

Carolyn is driving my mom, dad, and Susie in my car to the camp. The three-hour drive from Toronto must feel like the longest trip imaginable. It must be horrendous knowing that they must tell Josh and Gabi how critical

Steve is and that his chance of surviving is minimal. From what I know of my mom, she is likely trying to lighten the mood by chatting about the camp, food, and other trivial things. She is the eternal optimist; the art of distraction is one of her talents. I imagine that she is making everyone feel safe, telling them that somehow things will all work out. I am lucky in these terrible circumstances to have my parents so involved, sensitive, and caring. My children are fortunate to have, in essence, another set of parents. I keep in contact with my parents the entire drive. I need to be reassured, to know where they are, to hear my mother's voice.

Maxine and I sit in a quiet room outside the ICU so that we can make phone calls. Mostly, we wait. Michael arrives, having left Toronto earlier this morning. We meet him outside the ICU. We hug and cry. There are only two people allowed in Steve's ICU room at a time, so Maxine goes in with Michael. When Michael returns, his face is pale and strained, his eyes red and puffy. We are all broken.

I am forever aware of the time, trying to work out when my parents will arrive at the camp and when exactly I should call my children. Time seems to drag. My mother tells me there is construction on the road, which means the drive is taking longer than expected.

I sit in the quiet waiting room, picturing my white SUV on the road to camp. I know that route well. I can almost see my car, the road, and the camp ahead. I should be in that car. Normally that drive is one of excitement, but this time it will be anything but. I call my mom again. She tells me that they have just arrived at the camp gates. Josh and Gabi's unit heads are there to greet them, to guide them to Mark's cottage. Carolyn waits outside with some of Josh and Gabi's friends. Susie and my parents go inside. For the next twenty minutes or so, I sit waiting, agitated, and imagining what is happening so far away, while my kids and my parents share what can only be described as a nightmare experience.

My parents are already in the cottage when Josh and Gabi come in with their unit heads.

Later, my mother tells me that my children were confused and afraid to ask why everyone is there to talk to them. They sit down hesitantly, not saying a word, as my mom, in the calmest manner explains to them what has happened. She's overly positive about Steve's chances of survival and conveys confidence, reassurance, and calm. She tells them that although their dad has deteriorated, he is in good hands with Paul and an excellent medical team working on him. She is general in her information sharing and stresses that Stephen has a 50% chance that he will be all right. Josh and Gabi are quiet, teary, and shocked. Their grandparents hug and comfort them.

My mom calls so I can speak to Josh and Gabi. I try to stay composed, as I talk to them on speakerphone. Briefly explaining how Steve has deteriorated, I tell them that he is on life support, unconscious, and holding his own for now. I tell them that I don't know what will happen, even though I am feeling extremely pessimistic about his survival and outcome. There is pain and sadness in their soft, broken voices. They are so quiet and confused about what to do or say next. My mom asks them if they have any questions. They nod their heads no and sit quietly absorbing what they've just heard.

I realize it is up to me to help guide them. I say, "I think you should stay at camp for now, with everyone who cares about you. Keep yourselves as busy and distracted as possible. When we know more, we can make better decisions. Know how much Dad and I love you and somehow we will get through this as a family."

I don't believe they can think this through yet or really grasp the severity of the situation.

I promise to keep them updated with calls and texts. I ask them to talk this through with Gran and Gramps and make decisions that will allow them to feel more secure. Regardless of Steve's outcome, this trauma will change all of us. I know this for sure. I put down the phone and for the first time since Steve's accident, I sob uncontrollably.

Whatever happens, I'm going to stay here in Vancouver with Steve. Even though I want more than anything to be with my children, for their sake and mine, I don't want Josh and Gabi to see their dad like this. I believe that the lasting image they should have of him is the strong, energetic, and healthy father they have always known.

Initially, I didn't doubt this decision, despite the criticism that I have since received. How does one know, when making such an enormous decision, if it is the right thing? Should I have told Josh and Gabi to come to Vancouver as soon as possible? They would have followed my lead. But I didn't because I thought I was sparing them from trauma. I thought I was protecting them. However, maybe they needed to be with Steve and me, to share the experience together, to say their goodbyes if necessary. Maybe I made a grave mistake. If things had turned out differently, they never would have forgiven me. While I can't turn back time, I can reflect on my actions.

Later that afternoon, Paul arrives, and it is reassuring to have him here. He is embraced by the critical care doctors and made to feel like part of the team. He will ensure that Steve receives the best of care (not that he wouldn't have anyways). While the medical team is exceptional, they include us in all medical decisions and discuss every development and setback, they can't give us the information we crave most of all— whether Steve will live and, if he does survive, what the outcome will be. The new information is so complex, especially with my lack of sleep and heightened emotions, and I'm fortunate to have Paul here, who explains Steve's condition to me, so that I can better process what the medical team is saying.

Still, there are so many unknowns, so many questions. Is Steve getting enough blood and oxygen to his brain or is he hypoxic, which will lead to brain damage? What is his neurological function? Will he ever be able to walk, feed himself, work? If he lives, will he be on dialysis forever? Will his heart and lungs recover?

We stay through the afternoon, observing Steve and interacting with the nurses. Paul and Michael are hungry and want dinner. We head to a popular restaurant, just a ten-minute walk from the hospital. I go with them only because I'm too anxious to stay alone but when we arrive, I wish I wasn't there. I can't cope with a noisy, public environment. Of course, I also can't cope with being in a quiet, secluded waiting room, alone with my thoughts. I guess I just can't cope.

Paul, Michael, and Maxine order their food as well as something for me even though I have no appetite. The other people in the restaurant chat as if it's a normal day. I want to shout out that it's unfair, that my life is chaotic, and that my world is falling apart. I want to leave the restaurant, leave Vancouver, and leave this insanity, and go back home where it's safe. I want to close my eyes and make this all go away.

After dinner, we walk back to the hotel. It is summer in Vancouver, a busy tourist season, and all the hotels are booked in advance. We can't get another room in our hotel for Paul and Michael tonight, so the four of us share one room. Under normal conditions this would be quite humorous. Maxine and I haven't shared a room with our brothers since we lived in our parents' homes. It's all so bizarre. Worse, Michael and Paul are tall, big men. We have four adults and two small double beds. Maxine and I share one bed and Paul and Michael the other. Or at least they try to, but the two men are too large and so we arrange a single cot for Paul.

I lie in bed unable to sleep, trying to make sense of the absolute disaster my life has become. I feel broken, as if I'm teetering on the edge of sanity. How would my mom cope? She approaches every predicament with the saying, "*Ons kan altyd a plan maak*," an Afrikaans maxim meaning one can always make a plan. But how can I plan? What is under my control? What can I do to enable us to get through this horrific experience?

It's at this exact moment that I decide I'm going to take control of our future. I'm going to be an active participant and advocate in Steve's care plan. I'm going to tackle his health as if I am working at the hospital, as if Steve is my patient. This becomes my defence mechanism, my coping resource. This decision allows me to cope and prevents me from becoming immobilized with fear to think clearly. This is an active decision I am making, the choice to move forward, to think positively, to avoid drowning in misery.

From this point onwards, I become extremely vigilant, always observing, researching, and discussing matters with the specialists and Paul. I am always "on call." I am on a mission to do everything I can for Steve's best outcome (if he survives), as I owe that to him and to us all. I become a walking database, his medical/patient advocate, his case manager.

I need to know every medication, the dose, the possible side effects, the procedures, the measurements, and the results. I learn how ECMO, ventilation, central lines, and dialysis work. I know his serum creatinine and blood urea nitrogen levels, which are high, indicating severe kidney dysfunction. I follow his hourly and daily vital signs, used to measure the body's basic functions. This includes his body temperature, blood pressure, heart rate, and breathing rate. I store the numbers in my head; it's remarkable that I never have to write them down. I recall every number, procedure, and result, as if his life depends on them, which, of course, in a very real way, they do.

In my life before his accident, I struggled with recalling familiar telephone numbers. Now I can recite his body temperature to the tenth of a degree. The effects of adrenaline and anxiety have thrown me into survival mode, which has increased my cognitive efficiency.

The doctors and nurses consult with me on everything and designate me as Steve's "personal physician assistant." This becomes my full-time job. For the rest of Steve's hospitalization, I focus on his medical condition, nutrition, personal hygiene, clinical symptoms and signs, movement, and progress or lack thereof. I advocate on Steve's behalf, not letting one thing slip by, not being intimidated by anyone, and ensuring that his dignity remains intact. I try to conduct myself in the most polite and respectful way. But I am an advocate to be reckoned with. I have to be. There is no alternative and no one else to do it.

Amidst it all, I am deluged with texts, calls, emails, and Facebook messages, all from people who want to know how Steve is doing. Now that the kids have been brought into the loop, I can share Steve's medical status with other family members and friends who care about him. In an email on July 21, I keep things simple: *Steve is not doing well at all. He is now critical.*

The support we receive is both inspiring and comforting. Our friend Leora, knowing how anxious I am about Josh and Gabi, writes back with an update about them. Her children are at the same camp. She reassures me that my kids are managing as best as they can and are reaching out their friends. She tells me that Josh is coping well and is not shying away from talking to people. He wants to be strong for all of us. She says he's still capable of cracking jokes and participating in camp events. Gabi is quietly coping by hanging out in the cabin with her close friends. They are taking cues from her and talking when she feels like talking.

It's so beneficial for me to get feedback like this, to know that my kids have support. I'm glad that they are staying at camp for now, despite missing them and wanting to be with them. I tell Leora that if Steve survives this, he is going to need his friend Rob (Leora's husband). Leora and her twin sister Linda have known my kids since they were little. Tomorrow is visitors' day at camp, and this will be the first year that Steve and I won't be there. I feel sick for my children. Leora and Linda promise to take care of Josh and Gabi, and I am so grateful for this.

I desperately want to go home to be with my children and my parents. We need to spend time together, comfort each other, and work out how to approach the next few weeks. But how can I leave Steve? I wish I could be in two places at once, to support both Steve and my children. This is all so hard and unfair.

CHAPTER 7

From July 23/ forty-eight hours on ECMO and surgery to remove the ECMO, to July 27

FINALLY, FORTY-EIGHT hours after going on ECMO, we receive some unexpected good news. The medical team has decided to wean Steve off the heart-lung machine. He's making progress on ECMO, although his medical status is still critical. Incredibly, his body is sustaining and tolerating the treatment. His lungs and heart have now rested for two days. We know that the longer he remains on ECMO, the worse his functional outcome will likely be.

The critical care team and Dr. George I believe the time has come to remove the extra levels of life support. We are facing another critical decision, just like the one to put him on ECMO in the first place. These major decisions never end, and they never get any easier either. It's time to find out if Steve's organs can manage on their own. It is just over a week since Steve's accident, though it feels like a lifetime. So much is happening. Now that Steve is being taken off ECMO and he's headed back to the operating room to have the cannula surgically removed. I kiss him goodbye, not knowing if I will see him alive after the surgery. Waiting is excruciating, and as always, my mind is racing.

As we wait for the surgical procedure to take him off ECMO, I decide that I want to go home for a few days to be with Josh and Gabi. They need my support, and I need to know how they're doing. After discussing it with them, we make a plan. Rob will pick up the kids from camp and drive them home where my parents will be waiting for them. When Linda calls to confirm everything, I'm happy to tell her that when talking to Steve this morning, his eyes opened briefly, and then he raised his eyebrows, as if to say, "What the f&*k!"

Finally, the nurse comes to tell us that Steve is holding his own and that, remarkably, his heart and lungs are functioning independently. It's amazing that Steve has come through this. Once again, he's beating the odds. He has survived the accident, the risky transfer into the truck, the massive pulmonary embolisms, multiple organ failure, surgery to go on ECMO, forty-eight hours on ECMO, and now the shock to his system of coming off it. That's not to say he's out of the woods just yet; in fact, he remains in critical condition. But he's making progress. He's able to return to his ICU room. Most of all, he's alive. All of this gives me the confidence to leave him for a few days and go home to my children.

Amidst all the machines, he seems to be pulling through. Today, he shows brief periods of alertness and is even somewhat responsive. He is still unable to talk, due to the oral intubation used for the ventilator. He looks so scared and confused and it's heartbreaking. I keep gently explaining what has happened to him and where he is. I sit for hours, holding his hand, stroking his forehead, telling him how much he is loved and needed. His face seems to relax, and he falls back to sleep quickly. He sleeps for most of the day.

We received other good news today: Steve has been approved for transfer to Sunnybrook Health Sciences Centre in Toronto. He is still much too sick to go immediately but at least we can start the process. We are fortunate to have a good friend, Illana, who works there as a senior trauma social worker, help facilitate the transfer. What a relief it will be to eventually have Steve back in Toronto, near family and friends.

Later that night, Steve's brother Michael and I take the red-eye flight to Toronto. Paul will stay a few more days and Steve's older sister, Beulah, will arrive from South Africa tomorrow. It's reassuring to know that Steve won't be alone. If he is indeed aware, I trust that he will feel Beulah's presence, her calming, maternal manner, and know that he is cared for and loved. Maxine will leave to go home as Beulah arrives. Even though I promised I wouldn't leave him, I am, for my children, and leaving his side is devastating.

It's now nine days after Steve's accident and I'm on a plane back home. When I arrive in Toronto, I receive an email from the directors of Camp Manitou describing how Josh and Gabi are coping. I am grateful knowing they are surrounded by such compassionate and supportive staff and friends. I am assured that they have been participating in camp activities and seem to be coping well. They just left camp and I was told that it was a "beautiful thing" to see a large group of their friends walk them to the camp gate and hug them goodbye.

My parents meet me at the airport. It feels comforting to be with them, to feel their support and be in their presence. When I see my parents and we hug, I have tears in my eyes. I'm trying hard to keep my emotions intact and feel I must cope. I fill them in on all that's happened since we last spoke. At home, I am overwhelmed with the incredible support from family, friends, and our community. My fridge is stocked with food, there are "care packages" waiting for me and the kids, and there are countless offers of help. We are supported and loved.

It has been a month since I last saw my children. This will not be our usual exciting reunion but rather an essential time for the three of us to be together, to comfort each other, and to talk through our trying circumstances.

Gabi texts me to let me know that they are five minutes away. I stand at our door anxiously waiting for them to arrive. This time there is no welcome-home poster with smiley faces on the front door—just the tired, sad face of their mother. We hug, tears rolling down our faces, relieved to be together. We are exhausted and at a loss for words. They are suntanned and healthy despite their faces having a sad and worried expression.

I explain that their dad is making a little progress each day and that we will know more with time. I decide not to go into too much detail on this first day. I know my children; they don't like too much information at once. Instead, I gauge how they are coping and gradually fill them in over the course of the next few days.

As expected, Josh and Gabi avoid the topic of Steve's medical situation as much as possible. I think they trust that I am in control of the situation and that I will tell them whatever is necessary. I respect their need for us to be together, without too much emotion expressed or too much information shared.

As we spend the next three days at home eating, sleeping, and just being together, while, back in Vancouver, Steve is recovering from being off the ECMO. Gabi and I sit on the couch under a blanket watching TV, while Josh is on his computer. I'm sure their world must feel insecure and overwhelming. They are a little withdrawn, fragile, and at a loss for words. I try to realistically reassure them and provide as much comfort, without being too overprotective.

I am in constant contact with Paul and Beulah to receive updates about Steve's progress. It's July 25 and Paul tells me they are planning to take Steve off the ventilator later today. They will then closely monitor his ability to breathe independently.

With any kind of accident, and including Steve's pending transfer to Toronto, there's an immense amount of administration to manage. Legal forms, insurance forms, and as I begin to fill out what seems like an endless number of forms, I'm instantly overwhelmed. Maxine, now back home, and Phillip offer to take over these matters, relieving me of this extra burdensome responsibility. I am grateful that I can hand over our important legal, financial, and insurance documents to them without a worry. We are so lucky to have such continued support.

On Tuesday, July 26, we receive a phone call from Paul and Beulah with an exciting update. Steve has been successfully weaned off the ventilator, which means that he is now breathing on his own with the help of a less intrusive oxygen mask—a medical milestone.

Steve is waking more frequently, becoming more responsive, and is somewhat aware of their presence. Paul says that Steve is confused, although he recognizes both him and Beulah and appears relieved to have them there.

He keeps asking for me. Although I feel badly about not being with him, it is good that he is asking for me when he's awake, which is rare.

He remains in the ICU and still requires one-on-one nursing care. He has regular dialysis for his kidneys, respiratory therapy for airway management, and physiotherapy for early bed mobilization. His physicians closely monitor his medical condition, treating his physiological issues and helping manage his pain. He is completely dependent on the medical team for everything. He cannot move his limbs or roll independently in bed. His body is deconditioned with clear signs of muscle atrophy.

He is being fed via a tube, has a catheter for urination, and is in a diaper for bowel movements. He remains at risk for infections. Although he is making progress, his respiratory and cardiac functions remain precarious. We still have no idea about any neurological impairment that may have occurred. Though it feels like he is making progress, he has a long way to go, and we remain unsure of the extent of his recovery and prognosis.

In the afternoon Paul calls with some rather remarkable news. Steve is now talking and he wants to speak with me. Paul and Beulah have explained to Steve that I was at the hospital with him but have returned home for a few days to be with Josh and Gabi.

I put the phone on speaker so that Josh and Gabi can hear his voice. He says, "Dans, I'm good. Beulah and Paul are with me."

It is a voice I do not recognize. The effect of the oral ventilation has left him hoarse and breathy. He doesn't have the strength to project his voice, which comes out no louder than a whisper. "When are you coming here? I can't wait to see you. When you come here, I'm going to be fine, I promise."

We all have tears in our eyes. He doesn't sound like himself and it's hard for all of us. But still, he is talking. It is so great to hear him communicate. We speak for a few minutes, though I do most of the talking. I fill him in on the kids and I ask him a few questions. I can hear how tired he is; his speech starts to fade. There is none of the usual humour, wit, or life in his voice. He sounds depleted, even scared. Nevertheless, this is a step forward. I hope this continues. Unfortunately, I've come to learn that recovery is not linear. For every step forward, there is often another step (or two) backward.

During my few days at home in Toronto, I keep in constant contact with the ICU nursing unit, the medical team, and Paul. They keep me completely informed about Steve's medical condition. He is continuing to improve and is moved back into the spinal step-down unit, in a private glassed room, with two patients to one nurse.

Apparently, the staff are happy to have Steve back in their care. Once again, we are incredibly fortunate in unfortunate circumstances. The ICU and spinal step-down unit staff are exceptional. We receive the most excellent, compassionate medical care.

Steve's transfer back to Toronto is still being arranged between the doctors at Sunnybrook Hospital and VGH. Dr. George I feels that Steve won't be ready to be airlifted to Toronto until early next week. Bedflow and the ICU at Sunnybrook are contacted to get the wheels in motion. I learn that this is quite a convoluted process to arrange. Illana messages me to praise the admitting doctors' compassion and ensure everything is looking positive for the transfer to Toronto.

It is now my third day home with Josh and Gabi. Tomorrow, I will return to Vancouver to be with Steve. Susie, my sister-in-law, is coming with me for a week. I have no idea how long I will be there. Michael has bought me a one-way ticket. We haven't booked tickets for Josh and Gabi, although that is still a possibility. We are anticipating Steve's transfer to Toronto will occur in the next week and then we can all be together as a family.

I sit down with my children and have the most intense conversation we've had since we've been home together. I try to be honest with them and update them about their father's current medical condition. I explain that it's going to be a long process for him to recover, that we don't know how much he will improve, and that we are hoping to get him transferred to Sunnybrook Hospital in Toronto as soon as he is stable enough for the flight.

The kids listen quietly and ask very few questions. We discuss their options. I suggest they go back to camp in the next day or two and stay there until Steve is transferred to Toronto. They have both been at camp for many years, as both campers and counsellors, and it is like a second home to them. I know they have so much support there. If Steve were hospitalized in Toronto, they would, of course, be at his bedside. I feel compelled to protect them from seeing Steve in such terrible condition in this early phase of his recovery, which I'm scared will haunt them. There are other options that I consider less ideal under the circumstances. They could come to Vancouver with me, stay in the hotel, and be by their dad's side in the hospital. Or, alternatively, they could stay at home in Toronto with my parents. But none of their friends are in the city; most of them are at various camps, particularly Camp Manitou.

Josh is twenty and Gabi seventeen, both at an age where I believe they need to be with their friends, who will be caring, supportive, and offer a significant distraction from Steve's situation. Camp is a safe place for them, where they have responsibility, activities, and companionship; all the things that can keep them busy instead of focused on the reality at hand. This is the option I want for them.

Although I don't want to impose my views, I strongly encourage them to go back to camp. I need to know (perhaps selfishly) that they are trying to get on with their summer as planned. I know that Steve would agree, and I tell them as much. I stress that if they return to camp, I would be happier and it would make it easier for me, as I could solely focus on their dad and not worry about them.

I emphasize that we can change our minds at any point and that they can fly to Vancouver whenever they choose or if anything changes with Steve's condition. Thoughtfully, Josh says that he feels he would be better off at camp for now. He knows that I support this, and I am glad he verbalizes how he feels. Although he cares deeply about his dad, he knows that camp provides a healthier environment for now. He also knows that this is what I want for him and he is trying to do what I think is right and what makes sense for me during this chaotic period. I respect and reinforce his decision.

Gabi wavers. She is completely torn, quite emotional, and anxious at having to make this choice. She is extremely connected to Steve and wants to be there to help us cope. She may also need to be with us for her own security and comfort. Gabi has difficulty making decisions at the best of times and is somewhat immobilized by this massive choice. I ask her to trust me, being at camp will be better for her, at least for now. While she agrees, I know Gabi questions whether this is the right decision for her and for all of us.

Josh and Gabi arrange a ride back to camp for the following day. I believe this is for the best, but I don't know if I am misguiding them. Perhaps later they will be angry with me and regret not being with Steve throughout his hospitalization. Although they are my children and I am trying to protect them, they are young adults. Maybe pushing them towards camp is a short-term decision. In the long run, perhaps it would be better for them to be with Steve and me as we deal with our new reality.

As with all my major decisions, I don't know if I've chosen wisely. Life is complicated. Decisions can be broken down into their parts, but life isn't black and white. There are rarely clear answers to life's major questions. What I do know is that seeing the kids has done me a world of good. It enables me to return to Vancouver with a renewed sense of energy and spirit.

We arranged that I would arrive back as Paul returns to Norfolk, Virginia, where he is on call at the hospital. Beulah flies to Toronto to visit with Maxine before returning to South Africa. I am incredibly grateful to Beulah and Paul for being by Steve's side when I couldn't and to Paul for his medical expertise.

I will be returning to the same hotel, the very same room that Maxine, Beulah, and I have stayed in. There is a weird comfort in that. I pack my overnight bag with everything I think I'll need for my stay. I plan to be there for a week or so before we are hopefully flown back to Toronto by medivac. Illana and the VGH staff advise me to bring only a carry-on, as there won't be any space for luggage.

I have been in contact with Steve's office. I have his laptop computer to take back with me in case it's possible for him do some work while in hospital. We don't know what Steve will be capable of, but I am taking it regardless. It never hurts to be optimistic.

With the laptop in tow, I only have room for the bare minimum, which under normal travel circumstances would be hard for me. Despite the chaos in my life, it's important for me to maintain my sense of self and style. It helps when my clothes look good, my hair is clean and shiny, and my makeup lightly applied. I always try to look my best and even this situation has not changed that. My full head of brown hair remains at its finest, not yet having thinned out due to stress over the coming months and years.

With my carry-on now packed, Susie and I head for the airport. My friends wish me a safe trip back, and they send lots of love to the "Bionic Man." We've reached the nickname stage. That can only be good news.

CHAPTER 8

July 28, back to Vancouver, his buddies arrive and who all leave by August 1

SUSIE AND I arrive at the airport in Toronto later that morning. I am apprehensive about going back to Vancouver, the hospital, and Steve. By coming home, I have lost my momentum. I feel like I'm starting all over again. It is daunting.

Susie and I get along amazingly well, always have things to talk about, trust each other with our fears and hopes, and laugh and cry easily with one another, and so I'm fortunate she's with me. Over the years, we have spent so much time in each other's company, watching our families grow together. We always speak about how lucky we are, as both friends and sisters-in-law.

We've always laughed at the image of us in the future, two older women, reminiscing about our lives, sitting on a rocking chair on a porch somewhere. In all our musings, we never imagined going through an experience like this. This wasn't part of the plan.

On our way to the gate, we pass by a hat stand. To pass the time, we put on a few hats. I'm drawn to a straw fedora and instantly love it. It makes me feel good and so in the spur of the moment I buy a hat I certainly don't need. For some reason, I wear this fedora almost every day during my stay in Vancouver. I get many compliments on it, which lifts my mood. These days, I take whatever pleasures I can get.

It is now the afternoon and after checking into the hotel, we walk up the hill to VGH, heading towards the ninth floor, spinal unit. I don't know what to expect. I think about my phone call with Steve, his voice faint, his thoughts confused, his breathing laboured. I'm scared to see him, scared to face our new reality.

The few days I spent in Toronto proved to be necessary. The time from the hospital provided me with family support, the joy of seeing the children, and a much-needed distraction from the intensity of Steve's situation. And yet, those days, which I so desperately needed, have softened me. When you spend day after day in a hospital, you build a steely reserve, a defense mechanism, and begin to feel like you can handle anything thrown your way. When you step away, you need to find your bearings again, like that first day back at the gym after the holidays.

We walk into Steve's glassed private room facing the nursing station. Dr. George I, a nurse, and a team of resident doctors happen to be in the room. Steve is sitting partially upright in his bed, supported by pillows. We look at each other for a moment, without speaking.

There is a huge difference from when I left him a few days ago; he is awake and no longer on the ventilator. In this quiet moment, I scan the room and take in all the information. He is still hooked up to his dialysis, IV, catheter, feeding tube, and other lines. He looks like a gaunt, older and somewhat disoriented version of himself, which is a lot better than he looked a few days ago.

As I walk towards him, Steve says, "Hi Dans, you look so hot . . . if I wasn't in bed . . ."

I smile but am quite mortified. This is not something Steve would normally say, nor shout out in front of other people. I kiss him on the cheek and take his hand. He looks at Dr. I, whom by now we are calling George, and adds, "Can you see how hot my wife is? Check out her cool hat. I'm going to have to grovel."

His remarks may be humorous to anyone listening, but this is not typical of Steve. He is a man of few words, making every word count. This is not his style of communication. He has always complimented me but not so publicly nor so brashly.

As a former speech-language pathologist, I revert to my clinical, analytical mode of thinking. Steve's use of language is reflective of a communication disorder. He's displaying clear signs of disinhibition, impulsivity, and the lack of a filter. He's likely sustained a brain injury. He's likely cognitively impaired. This is devastating. I can't imagine my incredibly smart husband being intellectually disabled.

Susie smiles at this sweet, funny, and charming version of Steve. The staff in the room also seem pleased and comment on how lucky he is to have me back. He continues by saying, "George, when I come back to Vancouver, I'm going to take you out for a steak, because we always pay back our friends."

It is evident that Steve is trying to express his thoughts and gratitude; however, his animated manner and inappropriate comments are atypical. In addition, Steve has no recollection that Maxine, Michael, or I were with him since his admission to VGH. He believes that this is my first time here and he is so excited to see me. Right away, I understand that this is going to be a huge adjustment to deal with these newly developed cognitive impairments subsequent to his cardiogenic shock, organ failure, and ICU experience.

As I hug him, I explain that Susie and I are going to be here with him, that I will not leave him again, and that when he is strong enough, we will fly back to Toronto together. I express how much Josh and Gabi miss and love him. I share what they have been doing at camp and advise him that they are going back to camp tomorrow.

His eyes mist up at the mention of our children, and he says that he wants to go home to see them. He's so depleted, so confused, a shadow of his former self, and I am grateful that they don't have to see him like this.

Steve's cognitive impairments are clear to me. However, because his many critical and complicated medical issues take precedence, the medical team does not focus on or even notice his cognitive/psycho-emotional dysfunction. As his wife, especially since I'm a trained cognitive/communication specialist, I am devastated at this significant change in Steve. He doesn't fully understand what has happened to him, let alone the implications and consequences.

Initially after my return, Steve's progress is slow, with limited physical abilities. We logroll him in bed (a maneuver used to turn him from side to side or completely over, without flexing his spine), as he is unable to move himself. Even though his spine is now stable, he is incredibly weak. He can now stay awake for much longer periods of time and can even endure sitting reclined in bed, if placed in a well-supported position, propped up with pillows. Once he gets used to sitting in this position, we attempt to further his tolerances. We sit him up on the side of the bed, fully supported by his nurse, physiotherapist, and the RT monitoring his breathing. It takes a village of staff just to get him to sit. He feels lightheaded easily and becomes short of breath. He has almost no muscle strength. He can't feed himself or lift or hold anything.

He continues to make some progress over the next few days. He can now sit fairly upright in a reclining wheelchair for very short periods of time. This is no easy feat. Not only is he incredibly weak, with significant muscle atrophy, but he also can't figure out how to sequence his movements or grasp how his body moves in space. We must verbally guide him, step by step, and we often have to rely on a Hoyer lift to move him from the bed into his reclining wheelchair. This mechanically powered lift hoists him on a hammock-like fabric and transfers him with minimal physical effort into his wheelchair.

A full team consisting of his nurse, physiotherapist, occupational therapist, RT, and I are involved in these transfers. As we try to raise the back of the tilted chair, his heart rate goes up, his breathing grows laboured, and he becomes dizzy and anxious. We coach him through this ordeal and when he struggles, we must lower the back of the chair for him to recline.

This is a gradual process. We are working to increase both the upright angle of his chair and his tolerances/comfort while sitting, while also trying to build his endurance and confidence. To motivate Steve, we come up with a goal, to wheel him out of his room and down the hall so he can look out the window and see the beautiful view. It doesn't sound like much, but it will be a huge accomplishment for Steve.

Three days after my arrival back, Steve believes he is ready and able to start doing some of his regular work, claiming that "they" need him to keep on top of things. His thought process varies from "What has happened to me? I can't do anything!" to "I have to do payroll now. Can you give me my computer?" I realize he has no insight into his deficits and has moments of paranoia, confusion, and delirium. His thoughts are disorganized and erratic. His attention span is extremely brief. His communication, at times, is vague and confabulatory (fabrications that one believes to be facts). Paul and I feel this may be due brain injury, compounded by ICU delirium.

Steve can't understand that he's unable to perform any of the requirements of his high-level finance position. He is frustrated and even irrational. He gets angry with me for not letting him use his iPad to do work, either forgetting or not comprehending that he can't even hold his iPad, type on the keyboard, or clearly see the writing. It is not until later, after formal testing, that we learn he has lost some of the upper fields of his vision due to his brain damage.

"There is a conspiracy against me." He says, "The guys in the office have a secret password that they deliberately are keeping from me."

"Steve, it's okay if you can't do this now, I've spoken with them in the office and no one is pressuring you to do your work or conspiring against you. In fact, they are saying take as much time as you need to recover." I patiently explain.

Paul sends me current research papers dealing with early intensive care unit-acquired weakness (ICUAW) and delirium in ICU patients; Steve is showing signs of both. Delirium is frequently undiagnosed, as the health care team tends to focus on more pressing medical concerns.

Some of the features of ICU delirium include impaired short-term memory, impaired attention, and disorientation, which develop over a short period of time and are present in a fluctuating manner. Steve's simultaneous cognitive, psychiatric, and physical deficits occurred due to his critical illness and the time spent in the ICU. The more we understand his impairments, the better we can address his overall health needs.

His medical and rehabilitation team are dealing with his physical weaknesses and medical conditions. Thus, it is left largely to me to monitor and try to manage his delirium, cognition, and communication challenges. His delirium manifests in many ways: lack of concentration, disorientation, hallucination, delusion, agitation, inappropriate mood, and sleep/wake cycle disturbance.

I am now his voice, his rational self, his advocate, his therapist, and his compass. It is all consuming, but I am well trained for this, and I know how to help orientate him. I reduce the noise around him as much as possible, increase natural light exposure at daytime, minimize artificial light exposure at nighttime, help him improve his communication and gently calm him when he becomes agitated and anxious.

Over the next few days, Steve demonstrates increasing awareness of his own deficits. Now when he asks for his iPad, I set it up for him. He is now able to type very slowly with one finger when the tablet is propped up. Though he's made some gains, he continues to struggle. He knows he wants to research his condition, but he demonstrates considerable difficulty in his attempts to communicate his desires.

On July 31, I take a photo of the computer screen which shows him struggling to make sense of and research his own dysfunction. This is what he types into the search engine: "design design fo posr injury living."

Although he has difficulty expressing precisely what he wants, his thinking *is* becoming more focused and directed. I ask him what he is trying to find. He says that he knows he is injured and has difficulty thinking and moving, so he wants to know what can happen to a person after an injury. I allow him the independence to try and research himself.

However, after numerous failed attempts he gets frustrated and gives up. I ask him if he wants me to explain to him what has happened to him and what is going on medically with his body. He looks at me and says, "No, that's not necessary. As long as you know what's going on, I'm okay with that."

I suspect he is scared to learn the specifics. He stops asking questions and defers all matters to me. He doesn't seem ready or capable of understanding the extent of his deficits, nor of guiding his own recovery. For now, it's up to the medical staff and me.

Rob, our mutual friend and Steve's riding and camping buddy, calls to say he's flying into Vancouver later that week. He wants to help Steve in the most constructive and simple way possible: to be his friend, to motivate him, and to give him hope that they will go on adventures together again in the future. Rob is a busy dentist, with many familial responsibilities. It's incredibly meaningful that he is putting his life on hold to be with us.

When Rob arrives, Steve's face lights up. This is his adventurous buddy and they relate to each other and talk in ways that Susie and I can't. Steve is eager to describe his trip to Rob and show him the pictures he has already uploaded onto his computer. A glimpse of the old Steve is surfacing.

Rob and Susie become our new team. They sit with Steve and me, chatting and sharing stories. I feel safer having them around. Despite Susie's discomfort in hospitals, she endures for Steve's benefit. She is forever straightening his pillows to make him comfortable, only for them to get moved, wet, or dirty within a short period of time. She is helping in the best way she knows how, with love and good intention.

The physiotherapist has asked me to get Steve a pair of running shoes to help with his rehab. She wants his feet to be in shoes, to help with positioning, weight bearing, and improve his proprioception (awareness of his body in space). We already sent everything from his trip home in duffel bags and he's been wearing hospital gowns, catheters, IVs, diapers, and compression stockings. Until now, we've had no use for anything fancier.

Thankfully, Rob's here to help us with this onerous task: buying shoes for someone with very swollen feet and not being able to try for size or fit. Despite his limited function and general lack of interest in his appearance, Steve is very precise about what brand he will wear—only Nike or New Balance shoes make the cut. This is another glimmer of the old Steve, who has always been particular about his athletic wear and gear.

Rob chooses a pair of Nike running shoes. I will always remember the seemingly insignificant details: Steve's muscle-wasted legs, white compression stockings, black running shoes, and bright yellow laces. He approves of his new shoes and we are delighted they fit over his swollen feet.

Hilton arrives the following day from Chicago. Steve and Hilton have known each other since childhood. He has driven to Vancouver for the sole purpose of spending some time with Steve. Hilton walks into Steve's room and shouts "Kappy," Steve's childhood nickname. Steve appears excited (in a muted Steve kind of way), though a bit confused to see his friend; he says, "Hilt, what are you doing here?"

It's incredibly comforting and motivating for Steve to see his friends. He desperately needs some male bonding time, privacy, and a sense of control, as well as some much-needed time away from his "overprotective" wife. Steve has always been an extremely independent man, with traditionally male interests and activities, He often regarded my concern as fussing and coddling. He enjoys his time with his buddies, is animated talking about his trip, and participates in the conversation. They stay a few hours and then leave as Steve's eyes get heavy and he is ready for his nap. His days are growing fuller, but they are incredibly draining.

During our many hours together, I have noticed that as Steve improves in some regards, he continues to struggle in others. I am fully convinced that he is suffering from post-traumatic stress disorder (PTSD) and post-ICU psychosis. He has been experiencing hallucinations and nightmares and now that he is feeling physically stronger and sharper, he is able to describe these terrifying moments.

One morning about a week or so after coming off ECMO, he tells me about one nightmare he had, which he thinks may have occurred when he was on ECMO in the ICU, while heavily sedated. It involved Tiger Woods driving an SUV which was spinning chaotically in circles. Steve was on the back of the car, holding onto the rear-view window, panicked, feeling that unless he kept his hold, he would fly off. One could interpret this nightmare as Steve's desperation to hang onto life. Or maybe he had recently watched the Tiger Woods Buick commercial.

During these early weeks of his hospitalization, Steve is hallucinating and having delusional dreams. Initially, I have difficulty convincing him that they are not real. One particular morning, as I walk into his room, he is excited to share his "experience" from the night before. He tells me that in the night he had gone downstairs to the basement of the hospital to meet a group of injured bikers. He claims there is a hostel run by nurses, where many bikers stay overnight. He describes the room as being brightly lit, with amazing therapy equipment and contraptions. He said he was fascinated by this place.

One afternoon, Steve describes a specialized gift store in the basement of the hospital to Rob. He mentioned that they sell videos of motorcyclists performing crazy stunts and deliberately injuring themselves, and that the videos are fascinating. He suggests to Rob that he should go and purchase some as gifts for his friends.

Gently, we reassure Steve that such a gift store doesn't exist. That his dreams are weaving with reality and leaving him confused. He refuses to believe us and grows angry. We try logic. He can't move independently, and therefore it's impossible that he could have gone down to the basement of the hospital on his own. Still, his cognitive difficulties prevent him from making this connection.

Another hallucination/dream that he describes involves a person who had purchased up all the real estate in Vancouver. It's so interesting to see how genuinely upset he becomes, about something which would normally not affect him. He dwells on it for days and I think the person he describes to me may be the dialysis technician. He is confusing people in his daily life with his dreams. For the past two weeks, he has existed in a dazed state, and it is proving quite difficult for him to separate his waking and sleeping hours. It seems that his trip, the accident, the hospital, the staff, the TV, and anything else he encounters become mixed into his nightmares. He believes his hallucinations are real. It takes a few weeks for these dreams and nightmares to stop.

Though he lets us in on some of these experiences, there are other nightmares he never chooses to share. They are too frightening or strange to recount and he deliberately tries to erase them from memory.

CHAPTER 9

A few days pass

HAVING WORKED IN hospitals with spine- and brain-injured patients, it's important for the treatment team to see photos of Steve from before his accident. Seeing him as a person, not just as a patient, means the staff will relate to him differently. They'll see Steve as I see him when I shut my eyes: well-groomed, active, strong, and surrounded by family. They only know Steve as he currently exists: dependent, weak, sick, cognitively impaired, and physically debilitated.

Prior to leaving Toronto, I printed and enlarged a favourite photo of Steve and brought it with me to Vancouver to hang it on the communication board in his room. Steve looks healthy, handsome, and sexy in the picture. He's even smiling, which for him is quite rare. This is the person I want the hospital staff to know—my smart, athletic, cool husband. I want them to treat him with respect, protect his dignity, and be motivated and caring towards him.

While the hospital staff don't know the old Steve, his long-time friends Hilton and Rob certainly do. Over the next few days, they spend as much time as possible with him, talking, laughing, and reminiscing. They also look after me. They bring me food and take Susie and me out for dinner. I've started to eat again, and I begin to put on some of the weight I've lost over the last few stressful weeks.

Hilton will have to leave shortly, followed by Susie and then Rob. And it'll be me here with Steve again, by myself. I'll be sad to see them all leave.

But for now, they boost Steve's morale, sit with him when he sleeps, and chat with him when he is awake. When he's up to it, they push him in his reclining wheelchair, while manoeuvring his portable oxygen and IV pole. They are understanding of his limitations, while helping him work towards recovery.

Having Susie here for the week is so beneficial. I have a roommate, someone to share meals with and to listen to my concerns, thoughts, fears about the children, the future, and the impact of Steve's injuries on my entire family. She is empathic and compassionate. We also get to celebrate Steve's positive steps together however small they may be. She is here for me when I need her most.

Each time someone is here with us, they become part of our support system, our pillars. They help us hold it together, more than I could manage on my own. Both Maxine and Michael have said they would come back if needed. My mom also offers to come. The kids would come if I asked them. But I realize it is time for everyone to get on with their lives as much as possible. I am now strong enough to do this for Steve on my own.

Even though our friends and family are leaving, they stay in close touch. Rob continues to message me to ensure that Steve and I are doing well. I am happy to have some good news to share with him and send a picture of Steve sitting upright in his wheelchair. The photo means so much more to Rob than it would to others, having watched Steve in his struggles to get from supine to a sitting position. If only the photo had captured the snazzy shoes Rob picked out! Still, he's grateful to receive the pic and the update and wishes us well.

We have come so far. It has now been just over two weeks since Steve's accident. Two overwhelming weeks of crises, critical decisions, and devastating medical issues. Two full weeks of waiting, ruminating, and the unknown. And yet, somehow, we have endured.

Steve is now stable enough to move past simply surviving and to work towards recovery. I vow to commit myself to challenging and inspiring him to reach his full potential. Now that he is in recovery, I know we can do this. Steve is my responsibility, and I owe my husband—"my patient"— everything that's in me to push him to his limits. Having been through everything he has suffered, I can't let him down.

I shut out any thoughts of what could have been. I bury my anger, resentment, and sadness. I stop dwelling on the "what if" questions: What if he had died? What if he could never speak again? What if my family resented me forever? I do my best to stop focusing on my fear and anxieties, of his still uncertain outcome and the fact that the Steve I knew before may never fully return.

In the past two weeks Steve has become my full-time job, and I tackle his situation with logic, passion, commitment, and love for my family. I won't give up until Steve has reached his maximum potential, no matter how many times we hit the wall. I won't allow Steve to give up until we have regained some semblance of normality in our lives. I cannot quit until he can stand on his own two feet, both literally and figuratively. This is my goal and there is no stopping me. I know that we can do this. We have no choice. He's alive.

Steve remains on a feeding tube for nutrition, though we are told he will shortly transition to oral feeding. Survivors of critical illnesses suffer from marked muscle wasting—it can take years to recover. Good nutrition, particularly adequate protein, is essential for early healing and greater preservation of muscle mass.

During those early days, Paul and I discuss this aspect of Steve's case in detail, since this is a particular interest of Paul, while eating and swallowing disorders following neurological impairment is a specialty of mine. Steve is coughing on his saliva and most likely also on thin liquids such as water. Just over two weeks into his hospitalization, his speech-language pathologist assesses his swallowing abilities and together we decide to start him on a safer diet consisting of thick liquids with a pureed consistency.

Steve's respiratory status is still compromised and should any liquid or food spill into his airway, he could develop aspiration pneumonia. This risk is far too great and would set him back in his recovery. I know how boring and bland the texture and taste of this diet is, especially with hospital-prepared food. Still, we have no choice.

With the decision to start oral food, I want to stimulate his appetite and provide him with safe foods. I consult with his clinical nutritionist and then plan to get the most nutritious and appealing foods possible. Every day I walk about twenty minutes to Whole Foods to get him his "meals." Choosing his favourite fruits, I have a large delicious smoothie made, with high protein yogurt.

Steve lacks the muscle strength to suck from a straw. He also doesn't know how to sequence this coordinated movement. I feed him the smoothie with a teaspoon. It is a very slow process with limited nutritional intake, so it's good that most of his nutritional needs are still being met by the feeding tube. But we carry on. He clearly enjoys the taste of the smoothie and the stimulation in his mouth. To this day, he still remembers his ICU nurse getting him soft vanilla ice cream from McDonalds, claiming he has never tasted anything quite so good.

His dietitian monitors his nutritional intake as well as his hydration. As his overall strength, alertness, and cognitive abilities improve; his oral intake increases; and he's slowly weaned off the feeding tube. This is a significant accomplishment. I've reached this goal with many of my patients in the past, but it's an entirely different experience with my husband, one that I never could have foreseen or fully grasped until experiencing it together with Steve.

I am diligent about Steve's personal hygiene. It is imperative to me that he is clean and presentable as it makes a difference to how he feels and to his dignity and self-esteem. The nurses and nurse aides give him daily body washes while he lies motionless in bed. And every morning, as soon as I arrive at the hospital, I brush his teeth and wash his face. Every other day, I shave him and wash his hair. This is a new experience for both of us. The nurse gives me a special shower cap, sealed in a bag, which contains shampoo and is warmed up in a microwave. I lift Steve's head off the pil-low, place the cap over his hair and massage his scalp. I can see how much he enjoys this. When there are no shower caps available, I search through different units until I find more and shamelessly hoard my loot in Steve's room. After shampooing, I brush his hair and comment on how good he looks. This is a bit of an exaggeration. He remains so gaunt and pale, with a startled look in his eyes. But he looks better than he did a couple of weeks ago and so in my eyes he looks great.

During my time working in hospitals, I have seen unkempt patients lying in dirty or wet bedding. To the best of my ability, I refuse to let that happen to Steve. So I keep his bed fresh, clean, and dry at all times. I think the VGH laundry service will notice when we leave. Their linen carts will be fuller, and their laundry expenses will reduce. I have had full access to the linen cart, on all the units that Steve has been on. At the time, I don't realize what a luxury this is. In our next two hospital facilities, I need to plead, beg, hide, and hoard clean linen to keep Steve's bed to my standards.

Steve is still receiving intermittent hemodialysis, as his blood urea nitrogen and creatinine levels remain high. There is concern that his kidney function will not recover sufficiently. His kidney specialists (nephrologists) aren't optimistic that he will ever come off dialysis. Like so much about Steve's health, it's a waiting game. I check and monitor his levels daily, in the hope that the numbers will eventually come down.

He remains on a central line for his medications, including a heparin infusion to thin his blood. Because of his compromised respiratory function, he also remains on oxygen. There are moments when it feels like his entire body has failed and will never fully recover. Occasionally, we receive better news. We are relieved that his liver is showing signs of repair, with his enzyme level becoming less elevated.

Despite his acute medical status, he is making slow, but measurable progress. He is eating soft pureed food, with McDonald's soft-served ice cream remaining as his favourite treat. He is sitting for longer periods in his reclining wheelchair, tolerating the backrest being gradually raised to a more upright position. His endurance and tolerances are slowly improving; his vital signs are more stable; his breathing is better, and his heart rate is slightly lower.

He is making physical gains too. He is starting to hold a cup and other light utensils in his hand. He is beginning to participate more in his physiotherapy sessions. The physiotherapist and occupational therapist are teaching him how to move more functionally in bed, to become more active in his transfers and to feel more confident sitting on the side of the bed and in his wheelchair.

These small improvements ease my stress level and leave me optimistic. No matter how small his progress, each gain reinforces my sense of hope.

As a clinician, I know we have a long road ahead and should temper my optimism, yet I celebrate each milestone just the same. Despite his gains, the process of recovery is not linear. There are highs and lows, progress and setbacks.

CHAPTER 10

Early August (1 and 2)
Two steps back

E ACH DAY WE face a different situation and must navigate through a mountain of logistical and medical concerns. At this point, although Steve is making some progress, it's slow and in small increments. I need to remain motivated, for both of us, even if at times I'm disillusioned and despondent. The continual emails from concerned and supportive family and friends keep me going. My support network props me up when I'm feeling down and cheers us on when I have good news to report.

It is now just over two weeks into his hospital stay and Steve takes a turn. His respiration is laboured and he requires chest physiotherapy. His white blood cell count is up, and he may have fluid retention in his right lung. They send him for a chest X-ray. The doctors put him on new medication and schedule him for a CT scan and I encourage him to do deep breathing exercises to help expand his lungs. We spend a tense day together.

When I arrive at the hospital the following morning, my heart sinks. The nurses are concerned by Steve's deteriorating symptoms and they have paged the medical team. He has developed stomach pain, shortness of breath, decreased blood pressure, and low hemoglobin. He is lightheaded, weaker, less alert. There appears to be some bruising near his belly button. The team transfers him back to the ICU for further assessment and treatment. The doctors examine him and are concerned he may be bleeding internally but aren't sure exactly where or why. They push up his CT scan.

I accompany Steve as far as I can when he goes for the scan but must remain in the radiology waiting area during the procedure. My panic from the past few weeks resurfaces and scattered, frantic thoughts flood my mind. I don't know if Steve, or I for that matter, can withstand another setback.

The critical care resident says that it may take a while. Steve will go back to the ICU once they know what the issue is. He suggests I take a break and says that someone will call me as soon as they know the results of the scan. I take a walk as a distraction from the endless waiting. I need some fresh air to clear my thoughts and deal with my increasing apprehension.

About thirty minutes later, the resident calls me. "Danielle, we need you back at the hospital as soon as possible. We need you to sign consent for surgery. We have to reinsert the IVC filters. Steve is bleeding into his stomach from the heparin infusion and we need to stop it."

Steve has developed a retroperitoneal bleed that's thought to have originated from the arterial puncture site, from the insertion of the initial IVC filter. The bleeding Steve experienced is one of the most serious and potentially lethal complications of anticoagulation therapy.

Racing back to the hospital, I curse the fact that I left during this waiting period, especially since Steve had shown such clear signs of decompensation. Shoving my way through the crowds of people casually walking on the streets and in the hospital lobby, I'm uncharacteristically impatient, belligerent, and irrational, because of my concern and fatigue.

I run to the elevators, screaming inside my head for people to move. I stand at the closed elevator doors repeatedly pressing the up button, as if this action will make the elevator arrive sooner. When the doors open, I rush inside and make space for myself in the crowded elevator. I feel a wave of relief as the doors start closing but then someone else presses for the elevator and the door reopens.

I stand in disbelief as people make space for this "intruder." I don't budge an inch. I'm frustrated, incensed. I am wasting precious seconds; seconds that could impact Steve's life. I can't help but glare at the new person in the elevator, my body language and facial expression conveying hostility. The other passengers must think I've lost what remains of my mind.

The elevator stops at the first floor. I'm frozen with panic and people maneuver around me. I'm cursing myself for not having just walked the two flights, but I don't know the route to the ICU from the staircase. When I finally get out of the claustrophobic elevator, I race down the hall and am met by the doctors, consent form in hand.

Once signed, I slide down onto the floor of the ICU hallway, the wall supporting me, my head resting on my knees. I try to catch my breath, exhausted from all the chaos. The stress of the last few weeks—this emotional rollercoaster—is too much for me to handle.

I'm on the edge. I'm losing too much weight, aging too quickly, completely worn out. I may be coping in the overall marathon of Steve's recovery, but at moments like this, when required to sprint, I hit the wall—in this case, both literally and figuratively.

Closing my eyes, I breathe deeply. Once again, I must wait. Sometimes it feels like it's all I do. Waiting for progress, waiting for information, waiting for the results of yet another procedure. I slowly work my thinking back to my baseline. I am on my own here and need to cope. I need remain calm, rationale, vigilant and be an effective advocate. I know it's now up to Steve's medical team to save him again.

The IVC filter is reinserted and Steve returns to the ICU. His heparin infusion has been stopped and replaced by a different blood thinner cocktail, injected twice daily. He is maintaining his blood pressure, and his hemoglobin remains stable for now. A repeat CT scan is done which shows a decrease in the size of the hematoma (a collection of blood outside of a blood vessel).

We are not out of the woods yet. There is now a buildup of fluid in his right groin. The doctors are concerned that this could be an enlarging pseudoaneurysm (sometimes called a false aneurysm), which is a dilated artery or blood vessel that can form after an artery is injured.

In Steve's case, likely it's the femoral artery that was injured when the ECMO cannulas were inserted. This could cause blood to leak and pool outside the wall of the artery. He is given an ultrasound that shows the hematoma but fortunately no pseudoaneurysm. It is not until much later that the hematoma subsides.

Two and half weeks after his accident, we've hit another low point. Steve's outcome is once again unknown. He is no longer medically stable. Here we go again. I update our close group of family and friends.

> *Steve is a little better . . . a bit more stable. He now has hematology included in the group of varied specialists following him. They are monitoring his ability to tolerate the small amounts of Heparin and watching the internal bleeding. He remains on his dialysis, which he will have again tomorrow!! He's still very weak and very tired. We had a frank talk this afternoon, which was hard for both of us! He's somewhat overwhelmed by his many medical issues and that things keep going wrong. This isn't easy for him, as he has no control over anything at this point. It's hard to see his struggle, but incredibly he keeps beating the odds! On a more positive note, he was up in a reclining chair for an hour and had some fluids, which he hasn't had in three days. They are just watching his respiration, as his right lung is still not so good. He may need BiPAP again or more help with his breathing. They just did a chest X-ray, with the respiratory therapist watching him closely. He was exhausted when I saw him tonight. Apparently, he is now the healthiest person in the ICU tonight, so you can imagine how sick everyone else is. I'm grateful we are over that stage and hope to go back to the spinal step down in the next day or so.*

I send out a general Facebook message, brief and to the point: *Unfortunately, Steve has deteriorated, is critical again and is back in the ICU. Will update you as I know anything further.*

I speak regularly with Josh and Gabi. I explain we've had a bit of a setback and we'll be in Vancouver longer than expected. Then I email the camp directors to update them and find out how my kids are doing from their perspective. I'm still struggling with my decision to not have the kids by our side, and this fear comes through in my email to the camp: *I don't want to make them too anxious, because they are so far away. I really don't know if I am doing the right thing for Josh and Gabi? I think they appear to*

*be managing enough with the update . . . maybe you can get a feel for me, as
to how they are coping and what they may need.*

The next morning Steve is back on BiPAP (for extra breathing support), and the staff say he may have to go back on ventilation if he doesn't improve. I'm unsure how long he will stay in the ICU. He continues to receive dialysis. His breathing is being closely monitored; his right lung in particular remains a concern.

He is drained of energy and very pale. Any previous spark or motivation is now gone. It's heart wrenching to see him so sick. He doesn't even have the strength to talk; he just responds with a simple yes or no. He gets irritated with me when I want to brush his teeth. I take that as a good sign, better than no response at all.

I get a message from Susie. I repeat Steve's words that he's feeling "shitty." She knows exactly what to say: *It must be really hard for both of you. You are so good at encouraging him. He has to learn patience, which is not his forte. Stay strong!*

I speak with his spine surgeon Dr. Robert L, who is always so thoughtful and concerned for our well-being. He suggests that I prepare for a long road ahead, with at least a year to measure his recovery. Twelve months. How can I endure that long? It has hardly been three weeks.

I try to message or call my kids at least once a day. Josh prefers to hear the updates from Gabi. He doesn't want to have long or detailed conversations with me. It's his way of coping. We all have our own way of managing stress and communicating. It doesn't mean he cares or loves any less; it's just the way he copes with trauma.

Gabi is more receptive to my attempts to reach out. In our messages, in addition to updating her on Steve, we discuss all the irrelevant and silly topics that we would under less serious circumstances. It is good for both of us to feel a sense of normalcy. We talk about *The Bachelor*, the Halloween-themed day at camp, and whatever else comes to mind.

It must be hard for Josh and Gabi to deal with Steve's health issues. I remain hopeful they can still have the best camp experience as possible, under the circumstances. They are so far away and bombarding them with too many details would be overwhelming. I provide what I feel is enough information, although I question, "What is sufficient?" I am honestly not sure.

Back at the hotel, I have made friends with the housekeeping staff who have shown me where I can do my laundry. I sit by the machines as they run. I have so few clothes with me in Vancouver that I can't afford to lose any. I may have to go shopping soon. I play the pity card with the staff at the front desk and negotiate a lower room rate and a free fridge. I buy a yoga mat.

It doesn't take much to put me in better spirits: clean clothes, fresh food, the ability to exercise. I realize how small and compact my world has become. It has changed so significantly from before Steve's accident. There are new routines and they haven't developed by choice, but by necessity.

Because the medical team is worried that Steve may have C. difficile bacteria, they have placed precautions on Steve and his ICU room. For two days, I've had to leave everything outside, slip on a gown and gloves, and then enter.

Fortunately, the cultures come back negative. We bask in the smallest of victories. I am so glad that this is now over. Remarkably, Steve starts to show improvement. Although he remains weak, he becomes more alert and his thoughts clearer. His respiration improves and he is taken off the BiPAP and once again receives his oxygen via nasal flow. This is significant as they were considering ventilating him again.

Later in the week, his physiotherapist manages to sit him up in the reclining chair for an hour. He even drinks a cup of a liquid supplement called Resource for the first time in three days. I force down a sushi lunch. Steve is not the only one who needs to gain weight.

Today seems hard for Steve. He has a "deer in the headlights" look on his face. I acknowledge how low he must be feeling, encourage him to understand that his situation is slowly improving, and let him know that hopefully soon we will return to the spinal step-down unit. It's frustrating that our goal is somewhere that we've already been, returning instead of being able to return to Toronto.

I update my group chat with his progression. Maxine is considering returning to Vancouver to be with us and I do my best to provide an updated timeline. Unfortunately, Steve's recovery is so unpredictable that it's hard for me to know how he'll be doing in one hour, never mind one day. Until hematology reassesses his bleeding and hemoglobin levels, it's hard to know anything, let alone when Maxine can fly to us.

Steve starts making progress and is put back on the nasal prongs. He eats some solid food for the first time in days (blended fruit/yogurt). I bathe him in bed, shave him, brush his teeth, and wash his hair. I remain convinced that the better he looks, the better he will feel, and the better the staff will treat him. I joke to my friends that I'm providing Steve with a "spa treatment." The nurses are impressed and joke that they should hire me.

Unfortunately, Steve's recent setback has delayed our return to Toronto. The doctors (and Paul) feel that the longer we stay at VGH, the fewer specialties we will need at Sunnybrook. I trust the team here, as they have been through everything with us and understand the complexity and fragility of Steve's medical status.

I'm worried the delay will dampen his mood, but he starts asking about his motorcycle insurance and what has happened to his "beloved" bike. Even though his priorities are misguided, I'm glad to see he's still focusing on the things that were important to him before his injury.

Finally, the following day, we get some good news. Steve has been cleared to transfer back to the spinal step-down unit. I am so relieved to have the ICU experience behind us again. To celebrate, I go to Whole Foods and buy him ingredients for a delicious smoothie. I also pick up a salad and carrot cake for myself.

The nurses are relieved to see us again. We're happy to see them too, but mostly we're thankful to be out of the ICU. For now, things are moving in the right direction. We fall back into the same daily routine of shaving one day, hair washing the other.

The physiotherapist is slowly and gently moving Steve's arms and legs this morning. He remains extremely weak. She shows him how to lift his arms and legs on his own. When Steve tries to do so unassisted, it takes so much effort that his heart rate rises and we have to ease up for the day. Our goal is to get Steve sitting in his reclining wheelchair for longer periods of time, so we'll go back to this next session.

Steve rests after the exertion of the morning. Sitting at the edge of his bed watching him, I notice that he's making "pill rolling" repetitive movements of his fingers as well as subtle lip smacking/puckering movements of his mouth. He is completely unaware of these involuntary movements. I recognize these clinical symptoms and surmise the probable cause: Steve has developed extrapyramidal side effects or tardive dyskinesia from one of his medications. These are repetitive, involuntary, purposeless movements caused by the long-term use of certain drugs called neuroleptics (anti-psychotic medications). He's been taking Haloperidol to manage delirium. This medication blocks dopamine receptors, to diminish hallucinations, delusions, and unstructured thought patterns, all of which Steve is experiencing.

He's only been on the drug for two and half weeks, which means the symptoms are presenting sooner than expected. He's been so critically ill over the past few days that any "subtle" problem is easily overlooked. In the context of Steve's complex medical situation, the side effects from this drug may be imperceptible and not critical to the medical team, but they are alarming for me.

If I am not with Steve all the time, if I don't remain vigilant, his side effects will continue undetected, at least for quite some time. I call Paul, my medical consultant, to discuss the medication and its side effects. Then I ask the medical team to reassess his neuroleptic medication and/or to consult with neurology.

Steve's current critical care physician, Dr. Morad H, has just ended his on-call rotation, which is a shame, as I want to speak to him about the medication. The critical care physician on the roster now, who has taken over Steve's medical care, has a more abrasive and arrogant manner. He refuses to follow up on what I have observed and makes it clear that these side effects aren't a priority. In his opinion, Steve has more pressing medical issues.

The doctor may be correct that this is a lower priority for Steve, but that doesn't mean I'm willing to let them overlook the problem. I want all concerns to be addressed as they appear.

Steve is still having nightmares. His sleep is disturbed and he has extreme anxiety at night just prior to going to sleep. Simply taking him off the medication is not an option. I decide to leave the unresponsive medical team out of the loop, and with Paul's help (from Virginia) and the spinal team, we work on slowly decreasing the dose and then weaning Steve off the Haloperidol, while switching him onto Ativan for anxiety and Zopiclone for sleeping. Off the Haloperidol, his involuntary movements slowly dissipate over the next few days. I am so relieved to see yet another issue is now solved.

Even though Steve presents with muscle weakness and mild cognitive impairments, unfortunately, we never see a neurologist while at VGH. I believe he is suffering from neurological impairments, either due to a mild stroke or a hypoxic (lack of oxygen) event from the time when he had the pulmonary emboli, organ failure, and ECMO treatment.

It's Sunday, and things are looking up. Steve's kidney function is finally improving and he may not require dialysis on a permanent basis. They are keeping a close eye on his creatinine and urea levels. He is scheduled for another CT scan tomorrow, and we will then know more about the bleeding and the need for heparin.

CHAPTER 11

Still Sunday Reflection

I T'S HARD TO communicate critical information and significant decisions to people, particularly your family, from so far away. We all cope and react differently. My kids, much like Steve, don't like to initiate questions and don't tend to want too much information or too many details. But that doesn't mean they want to be left out of discussions completely. In my efforts to protect them, I am not always in sync with what they need.

Earlier in the day, I spoke with Gabi. During the call, I mention something about Steve requiring heart surgery down the line. She responds by saying that she and Josh didn't know anything about their father having heart problems. She then changes the subject and we discuss her camp activities and friends. Later in the day, I message Gabi back. I'm concerned about her reaction to our earlier conversation. To protect my children, I've been shielding some information from them, and I don't quite remember exactly what I have (or haven't) told them.

Sorry, I'm not sure exactly what you both know. There has been so much. Dad doesn't remember most of it, in fact he does not know he had a heart attack or has a ruptured heart valve. He asked me not to tell him anything until he is much stronger! So, I will judge in time when he is able to talk about his medical issues. Did I explain about Dad's heart issues well enough to you and Josh? I'm confused. I guess my reasoning at the time

was that I didn't want you and Josh to be overly anxious while at camp.
It has been rough, but it now looks like we've made it. I think I have been
protecting you both. So maybe I should have told you and Josh everything
earlier. It's not because I thought you couldn't cope, it's just that we are so
far apart and I wanted to be able to talk it through with both of you. When
we were at home, the three of us, so much was going on and we were all
still processing the ongoing changes with Dad. We spoke about his spine, his
ventilation, also when we thought it was pneumonia. Things kept changing
so quickly, with so many issues and so I think I didn't fully explain about
his heart. It's been a complete roller coaster! I am so sorry.

It is evident from my chat with Gabi that I am struggling to communicate
exactly what I'm thinking. I'm rambling, repeating myself, and not being
as clear as I could be. As we text back and forth, Gabi politely cuts me off
and tells me I've said enough and that everything is okay. She wants to end
the conversation as it's too much information for now.

Clearly, I have misjudged the situation and how much information to
share with my children. I now realize that both Josh and Gabi need to know
all the facts. They must wonder if I'm telling them everything they need to
know. When I do share information, they may not feel they are getting the
full story. It's difficult. My timing never feels right when I message them,
and I always feel that there is too much to send by text. But these are just
excuses. I have messed up.

I am unable to reach Josh and I feel terrible. I want to speak with him
and apologize and listen to any concerns or fears he may be having. It is not
until a year later that Josh tells me that he was upset and even a little mad that
other people were finding out critical pieces of information before he did.

Retrospectively, thinking about everything many years later, and taking
cues from comments that Josh and Gabi have made, I understand that I
did not necessarily do what was best for them. Maybe it would have been
better to encourage them to come to Vancouver and sit with their critically
ill dad. Perhaps I deprived them of being an integral part of his early hospitalization, recovery, and decision-making processes; after all, they were
young adults.

A comment Gabi makes (and Josh had intimated) compels me to question my parenting decision: "What happened if Dad had died and we weren't there to be with him?"

Unfortunately, in circumstances like this, we don't get an opportunity to go back in time and do things differently.

CHAPTER 12

A week later / progress

MESSAGE MY group chat, which now includes Gabi, on Monday August 8, with good news to share for once. After three long weeks, Steve is being taken off dialysis tomorrow. His creatinine and urea levels are down. One of his catheters was just removed. He's making progress and his critical care physician seems pleased. Steve has been sent for another CT scan and we are awaiting the results to determine if the bleeding has stopped. If so, they will slowly restart the heparin and monitor his reaction to it.

Steve has been receiving lots of attention, from his speech-language pathologist, dietician, occupational therapist, and physiotherapist. He is eating more, although not yet enough to meet his full nutritional needs. I head back to Whole Foods to find some soft, cold foods that he can tolerate, like Haagen-Dazs ice cream. Little moments like this provide him with so much pleasure. Steve tolerates being in the reclining wheelchair for about two hours today, which is a huge accomplishment. I help him with his workout because it requires so much effort to carry out even the simplest of movements. He is on 40% oxygen, which is better than yesterday, but still requiring breathing assistance.

By Tuesday, he's even stronger. His voice is clearer, and he even begins eating a little more: a scrambled egg and Pringles chips, the latter suggested by his dietitian as he needs to increase his salt intake. He has been craving Vitamin C water, and at the rate he's drinking them, I can't keep enough stocked in his room. I'm buying at least six a day from the gift store. His electrolytes must be imbalanced since stopping dialysis.

Steve continues exercising in bed and is getting stronger. He can now lift a two-pound weight and do a baby bicep curl while sitting. Considering he recently struggled to even lift his arms, this is a huge accomplishment. He laughs, "Who would have thought two pounds would be so heavy?"

He had an ultrasound this morning; this, in combination with the CT scan results, show that the two hematomas are slowly resolving. The team is monitoring this, so they can decide if/when to increase the heparin. The tests take a lot out of him and he's sleeping again, which gives me time to head to my favourite sushi restaurant on Broadway. The staff greet me warmly when I enter, know my order, and bring my soup and rolls to the table. Every day, I sit at the same table by the same window. I glance at a *People* magazine and stare out the window at the people walking by, enjoying this moment of peace, distraction and routine.

After lunch, I return to Steve's room to find him with his wonderful team of physiotherapists. Hillary, specifically, is the sort of practitioner everyone deserves. She is extremely committed, knowledgeable, and tough. She has a dry sense of humour, just like Steve. She totally gets him, and we are fortunate that she remains his physiotherapist throughout his stay at VGH.

My husband has come so far. Initially he lost any sense of how to move his body. He didn't know how to scratch his head if it was itchy, how to move the nasal prongs on his face if they irritated him, or how to shift his stronger leg in bed to get more comfortable. He was afraid to move on his own. He had lost the sense of his body in space, his proprioception. He was insecure in bed unless the side railings were up. He wouldn't drink unless the nurses or I were with him. He lost total confidence in his body and his ability to do anything on his own.

Over this time, I've been journaling Steve's progress: on Friday we had to assist him in moving his limbs (passive range of motion) but on Sunday he was actively able to move his arms and legs with support. By Monday, he could move his limbs independently and earlier today he started lifting two-pound weights. These are tiny steps but remarkable progress in only four days.

Over the week, once he is capable of participating, I teach him how to do simple tasks like brushing his teeth and encourage him to do it on his own, even though his muscles are weak. He needs help figuring out how to hold a cup and drink by himself. Everything is such an effort, a shocking contrast to the man he was before the accident.

He used to be fearless, independent, not needing approval from anyone for anything. Since the accident, he requires direction and encouragement to rebuild his confidence. His once strong body has been to the darkest places. He's been prodded; poked; invaded with catheters, lines, and injections; subjected to countless tests; has undergone multiple surgeries; and experienced a complete loss of dignity.

A man who likes to be in control has been rendered completely helpless, with a body that has totally failed him. I can't even imagine what this has done to his psyche. But there's no time to dwell. He is the Bionic Man and I am a warrior. How can we not make it?

Steve still does not want to watch TV, listen to music, or use his phone. It's too much stimulation for him. He says in order to cope, he needs his enviroment to be quiet. Hillary describes it as if Steve has been in a "cocoon" and he slowly needs to adjust to the world around him. We have to guide him and help him with each new step forward. We are his external GPS, his navigation system.

On occasion, I ask Steve, " Are you ready to talk about your accident or hospitalization?" He adamantly responds, "Not yet. I want to be stronger and healthier."

I think he is afraid of having more nightmares. He has had enough already to last a lifetime. He does, however, want to know about the matters that remain before we can return to Toronto.

He says he wants to be home with Josh and Gabi, our family and friends, and our dog Maddy. I assure him that the doctors and medical team here at VGH are invested in his care. They know the nuances of his injuries and have handled every complication. While I empathize with him about going home, I reinforce we need to stay here, at least until the bleeding issues are resolved. There are some benefits to us being in Vancouver. With just the two of us here, it affords him the peaceful quiet he needs to recover. It also allows me to focus on Steve completely without being distracted by our regular life and the inherent responsibilities at home.

Hillary works with Steve on trunk and pelvic tilt movements to increase his range of motion and strength. He does his first "scooch" and slide from bed to chair, using his arms to support himself. Hillary then wheels Steve to the gym, which is his first time out of his room in over a week. He feels quite insecure and over-stimulated, out of the safe confines of his room. He comments that it used to be so easy for him to multitask and now it's hard to focus on even one thing. Still, he's making gains. We meet Shannon, another spinal cord patient for the first time. I am drawn to his inspirational energy and his engaging personality.

In the afternoon, back in his room, Steve asks to speak with Josh and Gabi on the phone. This is the first time he will have spoken with them since his setback the week before. The call lifts his spirits but makes him emotional and homesick.

"Dans," he tells me, "I want to go home. It's been a long time since I've seen Josh and Gabi. I really miss them."

There are some insurance papers that require Steve's signature. His concentration has improved to the point that he can now slowly read and comprehend the forms and sign them himself. It takes time and a ton of focus, but we manage together. Then he nods off into a peaceful afternoon sleep. Today's physiotherapy workout has wiped him out.

When he wakes, I serve him dinner. His swallow function has improved, and he can now chew soft solid foods. True to Steve's style, his progression is quick. We transition from pureed food to tonight's feast of miso soup, roast chicken, and chopped potatoes from Whole Foods, with Haagen-Dazs for dessert. And then it's been a long day. Steve's exhausted. I stay with him until ten pm. He continues to be anxious prior to falling asleep. I help calm him, his nurse gives him his sedative, and I hold his hand until he falls asleep.

When I'm sure he's sleeping, I slip out of the hospital. I enjoy the fresh air on my face and the quiet in the dark streets as I walk back to the hotel late at night. I spend the next hour responding to emails, writing a Facebook update, and journaling my day. I think I'm mostly functioning on automatic pilot, unconsciously compartmentalizing my emotions, so I don't have to fully absorb the impact of our circumstances. I remain factually vigilant, yet capable of suppressing my feelings. At night, as soon as my head hits the pillow, I fall into a deep sleep. Steve isn't the only one who is exhausted.

CHAPTER 13

Almost four weeks after the accident / The end of second week in August (August 11) / Standing on his own two feet

ON THURSDAY AUGUST 11, I arrive at the hospital late in the morning after a leisurely start to my day. I respond to phone calls and emails, work out in my room, and take a shower. I eat breakfast in the hotel, which is a treat reserved for days on which I have more time. When I'm rushed, I grab a hot oatmeal from Starbucks. Today is an omelette sort of day. I order an extra portion to bring to Steve.

When I get to the hospital, Steve is glad to see me, smiles weakly, and says that he is hungry despite eating the hospital breakfast earlier. Wow, this is such a great start to the day. Then his face turns. "Dans, do you know I have a problem with my heart?"

His question surprises me, and I'm not sure how to answer. Until now, he didn't want to know any specifics about his medical details (until he was stronger and no longer at risk). What has changed? I reassure him that I know all about his heart and ask him how and what he knows. He says that one of the doctors has been discussing his transfer back to Toronto, telling the team that he will need cardiac surgery down the road. I ask him what he said to the doctor.

"Does my wife know about my heart problem?" he asked. The doctor confirmed that I do. Steve responded, "As long as Danielle knows, then it's fine with me. I don't need to know any more."

I am stunned because I have been worried about Steve's reaction to bad news, which might increase his stress, but he seems to have taken the news in stride. It just goes to show you!

"You have a tricuspid heart valve rupture, likely from your body impacting on the ground during the accident. You will need heart surgery in the future, but not until you are well and much stronger. You can exercise but may have to modify what you do."

I make a lighthearted joking threat, "It definitely means no more motor bike riding as a part of your exercise routine."

We laugh, and I note he appears to take this information well and then changes the topic. I am now relieved, as Steve, Josh, and Gabi are now all on the same page. Somehow, I'm managing to keep my facts and wits about me.

It is almost four weeks after his accident, and he is working hard to gain as much of his strength and function back. In the physio gym Hillary helps lift him out of his wheelchair, while Steve pulls himself up with the bars. He can stand for about ten seconds between the parallel bars, with Hillary supporting his torso. It is such a big achievement for Steve, standing for the first time in his new Nikes. It takes so much effort, concentration, and guiding, but somehow, he manages.

He cracks a rare smile. I feel emotional watching him achieve this small but significant progression, and for the first time in a while, I have tears in my eyes. He's getting so much stronger. He's eating more, very small portions, but with lots of snacking, Gatorade, and Vitamin Water.

Steve's newfound strength is shown in different ways. He has his own wheelchair now, which has been sized and fitted for him, and this is a great comfort. This means he's more confident in his ability to leave his room in his wheelchair. He no longer seems so scared and overwhelmed.

To get into the chair, Steve must perform a shift and pivot transfer with Hillary's support. He likes being in it and appears comfortable moving around. Everything is relative. In his previous life, he loved speeding around curved roads, low to the ground on his two wheeler. Now he's gaining some confidence slowly guiding his four wheeler through the unit.

Who would have thought that being in a wheelchair would feel so natural for Steve? He's learning how to turn the wheels efficiently, to create a roll and glide action, a more effective way of moving. Steve, who was such a skilled motorcycle rider, with many hours and kilometres under his helmet, is now becoming self-sufficient at rolling his own chair.

Each roll of the wheel, each room we pass, is an achievement. Once around the unit is not enough for Steve. We go again and again until we've travelled around the unit five times. This is the Steve I know. He's challenging himself, just in a very modified form.

We are attached throughout his journeys, as I follow behind pushing the Heparin infusion pole connected to his IV. There is a determined look on Steve's face, the feeling that it's good to be somewhat independent and regain some control, something he hasn't felt in many weeks.

The next time in the physiotherapy gym, Hillary has Steve stand up and down a few times, holding onto the parallel bars and learning how to support himself. She asks him to do baby squats. These are not the strengthening squats I know from my world of fitness, but rather gentle knee bends.

After that, she teaches Steve how to lift his leg, moving from his hip. She goes over where to place his foot and how to take a step forward. Despite his small, tentative, unsteady movements, these are the six most amazing steps that Steve has ever taken. He is so proud of his accomplishment, and I am his biggest cheerleader.

In the afternoon, after Steve takes a two-hour nap to recover from his physiotherapy workout, he wheels himself into his friend Shannon's room. They encourage each other and Shannon is so excited to hear of Steve momentous steps and squats. Only they can understand what it truly takes to accomplish.

The staff are amazed at Steve's current capabilities. On Friday, we are told it's time to start looking further into his transfer to Toronto. The transfer may come as soon as next week. Illana has been handling all the paperwork for his admission to the trauma programme at Sunnybrook Health Sciences. Today she contacts the Bed Flow Department to give them a heads up about the transfer and emails Lise, the spinal unit care coordinator here in Vancouver:

> *I know from Danielle that Vancouver General Hospital has provided the most exceptional care to Stephen, literally saving his life, and that to leave your facility will be tough in its own way. However, I know that coming closer to home will bring other relief for Steve and his family, and I am hoping that we can facilitate this as soon as it is appropriate and possible, bed wise. Could you compile the medical and care profile as soon as possible?*

Steve is now on the waiting list at Sunnybrook, indicating that patient flow is aware of him. However, the transfer won't happen until a bed becomes available. Since there tend to be many traumas during the summertime, it may take some time.

Steve is moved to the spinal unit today. We get the best room they have, with a stunning view of the Vancouver Harbour. I realize the evil eye pendant has brought him nothing but misfortune and it's time for another motivator. In the lobby of the hospital, I purchase a yellow Livestrong bracelet for Steve, which is being sold as a symbol of cancer patient support. Steve in the past has always admired Lance Armstrong, the famed cyclist, who has created this brand.

Early in the afternoon, our friend Lori, who lives in Vancouver, comes by with chicken soup. We are so grateful for the taste of home-cooked food. I am glad at how well Steve tolerates the visit. Earlier in the week, he wouldn't have been able to cope with any visitors. Today he's appreciative of the company.

We have a special Friday night dinner together, celebrating his move out of the spinal ICU. We have chicken soup, roast chicken, potatoes, and fresh orange juice, and we toast to his progress. Steve sits in his wheelchair and eats off a tray. His breakfast in bed days are over!

More good news. Steve takes fifteen steps with his walker, which I capture on video. He also has his first proper shower and hair wash since the accident, seated on a bath chair in a shower stall with the help of a male attendant. Steve beams throughout, claiming it is the best shower he's ever had.

Steve looks like a new man. We are finally moving forward. Some of his ICU nurses come to see how he is doing. He shows off his progress with his walker and they see a more animated, energetic, and determined man. The nurses are suitably impressed. We all are.

As he continues to progress, I find myself having time on the unit to talk to people while Steve is sleeping. Each person's story becomes part of our experience. Each situation is tragic, some with better outcomes than others. Time in a hospital is transient for most patients; although you bond quickly in such traumatic circumstances, you tend to lose touch as people move on. Will is young man who became an incomplete quadriplegic due to diving unknowingly into shallow water. Today he is being transferred to a spinal rehab. I wish that Will does well enough to live independently, that his girlfriend stays with him, and that his mom comes to terms with her son's situation. I must believe this will be the case; it makes me feel positive and have hope.

As I bond with Will and his mother, Steve grows closer with Shannon. They enjoy hanging out and talking about their experiences. They acknowledge how much they've taken for granted in the past, while marvelling at how incredible their first post-accident shower and hair wash felt. Simple daily activities like washing themselves or getting dressed require so much effort and concentration.

They laugh as they discuss how good it feels to accomplish what once seemed trivial—to sit on a toilet in private, pee standing up, stand on their feet, take a few steps, change out of a hospital gown. They talk about going with the flow and giving up all dignity, being seen naked, and needing help from everyone for even the simplest of tasks. It is a difficult adjustment for two previously strong, physically active, independent men; however, they are grateful for small achievements.

CHAPTER 14

Almost one month since the accident, August 13/14 / wind in his face

I T IS NOW SATURDAY, August 13, almost a month since Steve's crash. His critical care physician this week discusses Steve's imminent transfer to Toronto. He goes over many of Steve's ongoing physical needs, including how his anticoagulation medication will need to be monitored when we return home. I explain that Steve has difficulty dealing with the trauma of his accident and likely has PTSD. The doctor feels that Steve is currently too vulnerable, fragile, and anxious to cope with the extent of what has happened to him. He comments that we are not invincible, even Steve. He also tells us that the entire medical team finds Steve's progress quite remarkable, way beyond what they ever predicted.

Later that morning, Steve's spinal surgeon, Dr. Robert L, comes to check on him. He thinks Steve is looking far better than what could be expected, considering what he has been through. We all sense that Steve's condition, after such an arduous medical journey, is somewhat miraculous.

Steve looks so good that when we return to Toronto, nobody will realize the extent of his injuries. He's now in regular clothing. I take pictures to send to my group chat of Steve in black soccer shorts and a T-shirt. Still, the compression stockings remain, a reminder of what he's been through and continues to endure.

For the first time since his accident, I wheel Steve down to the lobby. For a brief few minutes, we venture outside the hospital. Despite being wrapped in a hospital blanket, Steve gets cold quickly. The wind blows in his face, and he doesn't like the sensation. It is too much stimulation for him, he becomes overwhelmed, and so we go back inside. The feeling of the wind on his face he so loved so much when riding his motorcycle comes to mind. It's a shocking, ironic contrast.

On August 14, Steve's running partner Debbie writes to say she completed a ten-mile race with Steve in her thoughts the whole way. She repeated his mantras: start slow; count the number of people you can pass; pick up your pace halfway if you're able. She passed eleven people in the last two kilometres, all while following Stephen's advice.

I read her message with tears running down my face. Steve used to be an amazing long-distance runner. Debbie, Rob, and Steve have spent so many hours training and entering races together. Steve helped Debbie develop her technique with the goal of running a marathon.

My heart breaks to think of what was then and what is now, from my husband running long distances to now struggling to ambulate with his walker. Although he has made huge strides with his walking, due to poor muscle control, he swings his right leg. He slowly moves down the hospital hallway, the intense concentration and exertion written on his face. This short distance probably feels like an ultra-marathon to Steve now. I respond to Debbie, stating that Steve is now "running" his own race and is slowly passing people in the hallway and picking up his pace.

CHAPTER 15

Home soon and melt-down (August 14)

L ATER THAT DAY, I post a simple update on Facebook: *"Home to Toronto early next week!"* What a momentous statement to post.

There are so many positive responses: *"Steve, you're a miracle man, clearly with a body and will as strong as can be"*; *"The hood misses you! Can't wait until early next week"*; *"Steve always started and finished fast"*; *"Freakin awesome! Tell the man to keep up the fight."* I read each message to Steve. He feels incredibly supported.

Before returning to Toronto, we still have gains to make. We work a lot on his walking and develop a system. I push the empty wheelchair about fifty metres ahead, and then Steve walks with the walker as I guide and reinforce each step. We work on how to be stable, how to bend his knee, how to lift his right leg, how to use his quad muscles, how to use his hip flexors, his glutes and most importantly how to take his time and not rush.

I stay at his side, talking, directing, reminding, encouraging, and teaching, while also pushing the heparin fusion pump. I'm sure he must be sick of my voice and my verbal cues. In our previous life, this may have been described as stereotypical "nagging, micromanaging, and controlling."—his perspective during any conflict that occurred during a heated discussion between us. But now maybe he's finally "hearing" what I say as he takes my directions in stride. We are a tag team now and no longer need the support of the physiotherapists or nurses to walk these distances.

Later in the day, Steve is wiped, so I help him get back into bed. I, too, am quite tired. The fatigue has caught up with me and his hospital bed looks enticing. So I climb into bed with him, he wraps his heparin line arm carefully around me, and we fall asleep together. This is the first time in over six weeks that we snuggle and sleep in the same bed. The first time I feel he is not so fragile that I can rest with him without injuring him. It feels comforting and intimate.

In the evening, some friends come to visit. They bring us a delicious hot pasta dinner and stay and chat as we eat. During their visit, they have been talking to us with Steve sitting in the bed, looking fairly normal for his hospital stay, which I suppose is a relative term. Then, Steve wants to walk them to the elevator to say goodbye. It takes Steve much time and manoeuvring to shift to the side of the bed and to stand up while holding onto the walker for support. He then must pull himself up straighter, while I rearrange his twisted soccer shorts, and we are ready to walk. He concentrates on the placement of his feet, the swing of his right leg, and his small shuffling steps. His gait is slow, he experiences shortness of breath, and he must rest after every few steps.

The subtle look of shock and concern on both of our friends' faces is apparent, despite their words of encouragement. It grants me the benefit of perspective. From my eyes, it's amazing to see Steve back on his feet and walking again, while for people who have only known the athletic, strong Steve from before, it must be quite upsetting. They must see him as weak and disabled. Yet he has come so far.

The ability to walk is a tangible progress for Steve because it makes him feel somewhat dignified. Hillary his physiotherapist, once said, "Does Steve do everything so fast? Is he a perfectionist, workaholic, speed freak?" She had him pegged from the start and we have been lucky enough to benefit from her excellent skills and experienced approach.

My good friend Linda messages me later that night: *I really realized through this how much I love both you and Steve and how lucky I am to have you in my life and I hope I can be a friend to you in any way you need me to be.*

As I read Linda's message to Steve, we both have tears in our eyes. Up until this moment, Steve has avoided talking about the emotions surrounding his accident and his roller coaster recovery. He has not been ready to cope with all the information and feelings, which have been building and building despite how much he wants to suppress them.

Tonight, all this changed. Our friends watching him walk with so much difficulty, and at one point losing his balance, has made him confront his situation through the eyes of others. I see the defeated expression on his face. He was so proud of himself earlier and now he realizes his limitations. It must have been crushing for him, the man who felt he could do anything, to appear so vulnerable. I empathize with him, trying to realistically build him back up.

"Steve, look at what you have been through and gained in such a short time. Your capacity to take on challenges hasn't failed you yet. This is one slow step forward, something you are not used to."

His response is simple. "Dans, this is so tough."

Then Linda's caring message about our special friendship unleashes an emotional response in Steve. The events of the day and Linda's words are a catalyst for Steve and the "dam wall" bursts. He is overcome with emotion. For the first time since the accident—actually for the first time since I met him when I was nineteen—he cries. His body heaves with sobs. I have never experienced this before with Steve. He breaks down entirely; all his defences disappear. All that fear, hopelessness, and exhaustion are released with his tears. I move towards him and hold him, while he sobs for a few minutes. I say, "It's okay to cry."

His crying starts to subside, and he wipes his puffy eyes. He can't look me in the face. I ask him to tell me why he's crying. He says, "I will never be the same as before. Simple things that I took for granted are so hard for me now. I feel incredibly guilty doing this to you, to Josh and Gabi, to everyone else. I should never ever have taken the risk. I should have known. I will never be able to do what I used to do. I feel so terrible for what I have done to you."

Steve is feeling guilty and despondent. I take his face in my hands and turn him to look directly at me. I simply and honestly say, "What is . . . is, and we can't change that. We can only move forward. You taught me that."

I reassure him that I will be there with him all the way, always. I empathize with him, telling him that it *is* scary now, that it *is* hard to do simple things, that maybe he will never be the same again. I say that our family will be okay and that we will deal with things as they come. I encourage him that we will work as hard as possible, to get to the best he can be. It will be a lot of work, but we will do it as a team. I tell him we won't give up, no matter what happens.

I wonder if my words reassure him at all, if he feels safe. I can't be sure. I would also choose to go back to who I was and how things were before all this happened. It's hard to accept change and limitations. I reinforce that he has every right to feel like he does, as he has been to hell and back a few times.

We speak about the progress he has made in such a short period and his growing independence. We both wipe our tears. I tell him that we can get professional support to deal with all his feelings and concerns.

Discussing his feelings feels like a huge breakthrough, in light of his PTSD. In the past, Steve never showed his emotions or his vulnerability. This previously invincible, independent, and confident man is now so vulnerable, afraid, and confused. He is a shadow of his former self and in need of help and support.

In retrospect, his PTSD lasts for a long time, evident in different ways over the course of his recovery. Initially, Steve experienced upsetting dreams related to his traumatic experience. He was unable to experience positive emotions, and he was emotionally numb for quite a while. For a few months after his trauma, he was easily startled or frightened.

Later in his recovery, Steve will experience irritability and mild angry outbursts. Because of the overwhelming guilt and later shame, he develops some self-destructive behaviour. He had trouble concentrating and sleeping for the longest time. The PTSD symptoms, overlapping with his neurological deficits, affected how he dealt with his traumatic experience.

After this one major outburst of emotion, he unfortunately buried his emotions and feelings again. He simply doesn't know any other way to cope. Later, he struggles with his vulnerability, keeping his emotions walled off behind a mask. Irrespective of his condition, he would force himself to believe and tell others that he was fine, perfect actually.

However, for a short period of time this emotional breakthrough helps him manage. After this discussion Steve is totally exhausted and ready to go to sleep. I call his nurse, who has worked with Steve many times in the spinal unit and knows him well. She is kind and reassuring and helps him prepare for bed.

She removes Steve's heparin fusion line, the last of all the lines and IV equipment attached to his body. This is a significant accomplishment for now and it symbolizes Steve's progress. He is finally free of lines, tubes, and any other invasive medical device into his body. This is worth a celebration. However, he is ready for bed, and drinking a toast to his progress can be saved to another time.

We agree that he is now feeling lighter in many ways. For the first time, he is given his heparin via an injection into his stomach. Later in his medical journey, this daily injection, as well as inserting IV lines into his veins, will create immense anxiety for Steve. But tonight, the heparin injection feels like a victory.

His legs are sore and he so tired, both emotionally and physically. But his face looks calmer and less afraid. His oxygen is placed back on for the night. He tells me that he feels much better now, and I am grateful for this breakthrough. I sit on his bed until he falls asleep. I feel relieved and pleased; we have accomplished a lot today. I head back to the hotel, completely exhausted.

CHAPTER 16

August 15 to 18— emails and trips

ON AUGUST 15, Steve wakes feeling considerably better. He's invigorated and excited to go back to Toronto. Yesterday's outpouring of emotions has left him feeling much more at peace. He decides he wants to send a second email to our entire network explaining his progress. Typing and concentrating are still hard for him, so he dictates the email to me. He called the subject, "Broken . . . but on the mend."

So, it's been a month since my accident! A lot has happened in that time. Most of you know probably know more than I do about what's happened. I have consciously chosen not to know any of the details until I feel stronger, and am further in my recovery. It finally looks like I'll be Medivacked to Sunnybrook Hospital on Tuesday or Wednesday of this week, all depending when a bed is available in Toronto. Illana, finally you are getting me my room with a view, even though it's not Baycrest, I'll settle for Sunnybrook!

So . . . let's go back to the last I remember, after the accident, where I was lying flat on my back, before my surgery in Vancouver, when I wrote my last email. Rereading that email, it seemed that I appeared quite lucid. Going from bits I've heard people talking, my first few weeks seemed to have been a medical miracle! In the last week or so, I seem to have turned the corner. From struggling to lift two-pound weights, I've now increased all the way up to 3 pounds. From not being able to feed myself, I can now eat most foods I want. Tonight, Danielle brought in a delicious steak salad, which was the treat of the week. I can walk with a walker, who would think that walking could be so hard! At one stage, there was concern that my kidneys may not recover, but in the last week everything seems fine. I sure have enjoyed my recovery by drinking gallons of Gatorade and Vitamin water . . . In a few months' time, we will drink a beer together.

Yesterday, the enormity of my situation suddenly hit me, realizing what had actually happened and what is still ahead of me! It's been the toughest thing I've ever done. I can only be thankful that I have Danielle to look after me, who has been with me through this. I can't wait to get home to see Josh and Gabi. It's been a long time away from home. Maxine, Michael, Paul, Beulah, Susie, Rob, and Hilt, I am eternally grateful for you coming to be with me. Colin and Jocelyn, I know how concerned you have been about me. Danielle has told me about the overwhelming support from everyone. The doctors, nurses, therapists, and all of the staff at Vancouver General Hospital have been excellent. Right from my initial surgery, through all the complications (and I hear there have been quite a few), all the specialists, with Paul part of the team, I hear have been amazing!

So the big question . . . after five amazing years of seeing North America, like I never dreamt I would explore it (been to Alaska twice, Northern Quebec and Eastern Canada, the Great Lakes a number of times, Tail Of the Dragon, Blue Ridge Parkway, Glacier National Park . . . and yes, even Sturgis, South Dakota), is it time to park the bike???? FOR SURE . . . It's time now to cut back on the risk and find a new challenge (less extreme!). More than 9 of my lives have been used up on this last little escapade!!

We get so many responses back, including these standout messages of support:

Your note is inspiring. There's a great old song with the lyrics "I'm not broken but I'm badly bent"—we'll try to find for you—time to get your smile and mojo working too. Looking forward to seeing you.

Bent but unbowed! Seems so to me, courage is spelled S-t-e-p-h-e-n from now on in our house. Thanks for the update—you know we're all thinking of you, and never doubting for a moment that you will rise to this challenge—Wishing you strength brother for those times when you'll have to dig deep.

We are all so amazed at Steve's recovery. He is truly a man of steel, not just the butt of Steel. We cannot wait to have you back :)

And from Illana: *Very relieved you are giving up the "donor cycle" Steve, as we call it here. And I can be of good service to talk to you further about your smart risk options . . . after all I have learnt in trauma here for the past 20 years, I am a wealth of knowledge . . . I promise to bore you to tears!*

We spend much of the day communicating with friends and family, reading and re-reading emails, and reflecting on everything that has happened. Steve has come such a long way. Some emails allude to the special romance and love between Steve and me enduring this trying journey together. I shudder at this concept. In my eyes, there has been nothing romantic about this traumatic and gruelling experience. We do have the deepest friendship, respect, love of family, trust, and profound connection. I believe our family and our bond will help us continue to cope when we are finally home. But nothing about this is hearts and roses.

The following day marks one month since Steve's accident. Steve is working on his arm and shoulder exercises while sitting in his wheelchair. Although it's still difficult for him and he tires quickly, becoming short of breath, he persists.

I take the opportunity of him being in a better headspace, of us being able to measure his progress and decide to share and clarify with him in some detail his medical circumstances, the events over the past month, and the plans ahead. I explain how seriously ill he was and that he required so many intensive treatments. I tell him that the doctors, nurses, and technicians are amazed at his recovery and that's why we keep getting stopped in the hallways by the staff to say hi and check in. The sweet and innocent Steve says: "Dans, I thought that you kept talking to all the staff because they liked you and that everyone is so friendly." I smile at his naiveté and wonder how long this will last.

As I continue to relay the events of the past month, Steve appears to be in a bit of shock. I can tell he's finding it hard to grasp just how critically ill he was. He says it will take time to process all the information.

Tonight is also sad for us, as we say goodbye to Shannon, even if it is for a good reason, as he's moving to a spinal rehabilitation facility. Shannon and Steve have fought through many experiences together. It has been good for them to have someone else who really understands their limitations and challenges and who has walked in their shoes. They have cheered each other on, laughed at themselves, and bonded over sports and pizza.

Later in the afternoon, we go for a walk outside with the wheelchair to get fresh air and a beautiful view of the mountains. We make a pact to come back to Vancouver, when Steve is strong and walking, to visit VGH and Shannon, and to enjoy the mountains and great food.

Tonight, Steve falls asleep feeling relaxed and motivated to work on his recovery. He seems at ease with himself, more animated and ready to begin the next phase of his journey. That "deer in the headlights" facial expression is slowly fading. At first, I had been worried to tell Steve about the course of his hospitalization, but now I'm feeling that the knowledge may be a relief for him. He again seems so much lighter. I think understanding his medical issues has maybe taken away much of his fear. The old Steve is on his way back!

Steve's medical team has been coming by to see him off. We take a group picture and have a great discussion with Steve's amazing spine surgeon, Dr. Robert L, and our critical care idol, Dr. George I. We are used to them saying hello, but it's much harder to possibly be saying goodbye. Worse, due to the uncertainty of the transfer dates, we never know if it will be the last time we'll see a certain special hospital staff member, and it's hard to fully convey our appreciation.

Until the transfer arrives, our days must carry on as usual. I buy Steve a delicious omelette and toast for brunch, insistent on fattening him up. He has an amazing workout in physiotherapy, walking backwards, balancing, and rotating between the parallel bars, all new accomplishments for him.

It is such hard work and requires so much concentration for him, but his efforts are paying off.

In the afternoon, we go on the most exciting adventure since Steve's accident. If you think riding to Alaska is risky and daring, it's nothing compared with our search for a fresh salad for dinner. Steve's sense of adventure is back, and against my better instincts, we navigate the steep streets for the perfect meal. I guide his wheelchair down the very steep hill for two long blocks to get to Broadway Street, a main road. I am so scared that I will let Steve and the wheelchair slip out of my hands. This is the furthest we've ventured from the hospital together.

We are quite the sight. Steve is dressed in his white thigh-high compression stockings, black Nike shoes with yellow laces and baggy soccer shorts. To finish the ensemble, he's wrapped up in a striped flannel hospital blanket. People everywhere seem to be smiling at us, either out of sympathy or to quietly cheer us on. A child comes up to us and asks if Steve has two broken legs.

Steve is thoroughly enjoying himself, feeling free and out of the confines of the hospital. He is tolerating the noise, the people walking, and the general activity on the road. He hasn't experienced this in over a month. He can now cope with the external stimulation around him. This is major progress. But I am breaking into a sweat, from the physical work and the fear that Steve is entirely my responsibility in this big, open, unprotected world. Wendy's restaurant is the closest place open for a salad and so we decide to go inside. An elderly man outside takes pity on us, opens the wheelchair accessible door, and then blesses Steve.

Steve is so excited to be eating in a restaurant, even if it's nothing more than a fast-food chain. He keeps smiling, which is so reinforcing, as Steve is not one to feign emotions. We order berry salads, set up at a makeshift wheelchair table, and eat our salads together. I am anxious that something will go wrong but happy that we have achieved this. I call our family to share this huge triumph. Michael wishes me luck getting him back up the hill, which I have overlooked amidst all the excitement.

While it is tough work pushing Steve up the hill to the hospital, I'm encouraged by the sense of accomplishment. We make it back in good time, laughing at my hard work, feeling my glutes and hamstrings being put to the test. It's another day and another adventure. I am so proud of him, of us both.

When we return to the hospital, I look further into the process to arrange the transfer to Sunnybrook Hospital in Toronto. The entire matter is really complicated. It is time-sensitive and we must ensure all the medical requirements are met. For the transfer to work, a bed at Sunnybrook must be unoccupied on a specific day, the medivac jet and staff need to be available to fly, the transfer from VGH needs to be organized, and Steve needs to be deemed medically safe to fly.

We speak first with Lise, the clinical nurse specialist in the VGH acute spine programme. She determines we have completed the required paperwork and contacts Illana to set the transfer in motion:

Stephen is ready to go when you have a bed. Please find attached his transfer summary. Let me know if you need anything else. We will be sending full transcriptions for all consults with Stephen. Let me know when you have a bed and I will call Manulife to organize Air.

Illana then contacts Patient Flow at Sunnybrook:

Here is the detailed summary I sent today. Lise identifies that Stephen K is now a ward level patient, stable for transfer. We should be able to expedite this, as the patient only requires a C5 bed now, no longer an ICU bed. We should have some of our traumas moving this week. Is there any sense of a possible bed for this patient? I would appreciate any update, so I can let this family have a general idea too. With thanks for your assistance.

Illana messages me privately and tells me that the trauma doctor is working to help things along. Unfortunately, there are other patients who take priority.

The head of bed flow emails Dr. T on Thursday August 18:

Today, we have twenty-two admitted ward level patients without beds. I appreciate that this patient is known to Sunnybrook, however Patient

Flow is directed to allocate resources to our daily intake of patients first. We have Mr. K on our list, which we review daily, and we have been in contact with Vancouver. When we have the capacity to bring him to Sunnybrook we will.

We've been so ready to head home to Toronto, but alas there is no bed available. I speak with Illana and learn that Steve's transfer is unlikely to come available in the next few days and that we need to be patient.

I have developed tendonitis in my thumb ("Blackberry thumb"), due to overuse from constantly texting, emailing, and messaging. As I deal with a minor sore thumb, Steve continues to regain his ability to walk. Today in physiotherapy, he's progressed to using specialized forearm crutches. It is unbelievably hard work for him. He must hold his body upright when walking, much effort in lifting his right leg, balance and coordinate his movements, all while using the crutches. He is still quite weak, yet he manages well, beyond what any of us expected in such a short period.

Today, just as Hillary had earlier, his new physiotherapist asks, "Steve, do you always do everything fast?"

This gives me a good laugh. Everyone who knows Steve well knows that he eats, walks, runs, drives, and thinks quickly, as he doesn't know how to operate at a slower speed. Even with his limitations and disabilities, he's on the fast track.

After his session, we have a picnic lunch in the small park across the road from the hospital. We eat with the sun shining on our faces. We feel a sense of freedom and privilege to be in a park, relaxing and feeling the sun seep into our tired and pale bodies. We decide to make the most of our extended stay here. I tell Steve that if we are still here Saturday, I'll take him on another big adventure in the world outside of the hospital.

Thursday August 18 marks another accomplishment for Steve. He is now totally independent in terms of using the bathroom on his own during the day. This is such a significant achievement for him and a huge milestone in regaining some of his lost dignity. Using the bathroom is a simple task that most of us take for granted, but this is a huge marker of progress for

Steve. To master the washroom on his own takes timing, strength, balance, and confidence. He is so relieved (literally and figuratively).

Steve and I have become familiar faces to many of the families and patients in the spinal unit. Often, they stop by our room and chat. It is a way of breaking up the monotony of the long days. Tonight, Sylvio, a trucker, comes by our room. He is in a halo vest to stabilize his cervical spine. He clearly needs to talk and share the details of his accident, and we happen to be the people available with whom he feels comfortable talking. We both struggle to cope with Sylvio's story. As Steve continues to suffer from PTSD, any traumatic discussion results in increased anxiety. I am afraid this conversation will trigger even more nightmares than he is already having.

I try to be delicate and sensitive to both men's needs and try to escort Sylvio out of Steve's room. However, Sylvio is adamant he wants to talk to Steve and sits down on the chair in Steve's room, refusing to budge. I worry that Steve may need more than his normal dose of Ativan to sleep tonight.

Sylvio tells us he was driving on a mountain pass on a quiet road when his truck rolled over an embankment. It landed upside down in bushes and soft soil, pinning him inside, with no escape. He tells us how he spent five hours digging himself out of the sand, with his one hand, so he could make a space big enough to crawl through and extricate himself from the truck.

I have claustrophobia and the thought of being buried alive fills me with anxiety. Everything at this point frightens Steve. This is not the bedtime story that either of us wants to hear, especially after a pleasant day in the sun. However, Sylvio needs us to listen and support him, so that's what we do. He continues to explain how he survives and makes it to the road with what must have been pure adrenaline and sheer determination.

Eventually someone stopped and called for emergency help. He was airlifted to VGH and thus we met. We have never forgotten his story. We have heard many stories from many patients at many facilities, but this one will always stick with us.

After having had a stressful evening with the second trucker on Steve's journey, I wake up the next morning to a message from Illana telling me they anticipate a bed for Steve. She explains the logistics and tries not to get my hopes up in case the transfer falls through. I am starting to get anxious as the logistics are complicated and the bed is imminent but not yet confirmed. I leave the hotel without having breakfast, both nervous and excited, and walk to the hospital to fill Steve in on the hopeful news.

I have a sense of accomplishment having stayed in Vancouver with so little clothing and only a small carry-on bag since my return from visiting the children. For the past five weeks, I have lived in two pairs of jeans, one dress, one skirt, a denim jacket, a few T-shirts and tops, two pairs of shoes and a hat. I feel like one of those models in a magazine that demonstrates how to mix and match ten basic items. In my head, I see the article title: "It only takes ten staple fashion pieces to create multiple looks for the holidays."

When I arrive at the hospital, I tell Steve about the likelihood of a bed at Sunnybrook and medivac to come in the next twenty-four hours. He is relieved and emotionally ready to go home. I help him get dressed; however, while removing his hospital gown, I notice that he has developed a small leak from the almost closed suture site from his spine surgery. I did not see this last night. I press my finger on the area and liquid oozes out. I am now concerned as I think he may have developed an infection.

We have Dr. Robert L paged. He assesses the leak and tells us that, at best, this means Steve has an infection of only the tissue around his spinal surgery site; at worst, it may be an infection deep in the wound. It appears that a hematoma could have developed over the wound as a result of the tPA.

My heart sinks. Steve looks disappointed and grows anxious. It would be nice if just once something with Steve and his medical issues could be straightforward or simple. Dr. L suggests we stay in Vancouver, so he can perform spine surgery to clean out the infection. He is very reluctant to let us go on to another medical team in another city, as he is fully invested in Steve's well-being and recovery.

However, this option would mean that we must remain in Vancouver for at least a few more weeks for treatment and follow up. I am totally prepared to stay in Vancouver, as I have complete faith, trust, and security in Dr. L. the spinal team, and all the physicians here at VGH. But Steve is quite devastated at the prospect of staying any longer in Vancouver and not going home to his family.

Emotionally, the return trip represents a measure of his progress. Steve expresses that this setback would crush his morale and he would not be able to handle it. Although he has made significant improvement and is not quite as fearful as before, he is still feeling insecure and anxious. Going to Sunnybrook Hospital is one step closer to being at home, to returning to his life as he knew it.

So, taking in to account his emotional needs, his inability to cope, his PTSD and his stability, we make a collective decision to continue with the transfer home and have the specialists at Sunnybrook take care of the infection. Dr. L explains that the spinal surgeons will need to check his wound and infection as soon as we arrive at Sunnybrook. He suggests that an incisional vacuum/pump be used to clean out the infection and that if the wound does not improve, Steve will require surgery. This would involve reopening his wound, cleaning out and removing some of the infected tissue, and using packing until it slowly heals. Steve may require strong antibiotics for the long term. I take in all the information feeling I need to relay this to the doctors when we arrive at Sunnybrook.

Even though I know all physicians in Canada are well trained, I am concerned that I may not develop a relationship with the medical team as strong as the one I have here and will have to work hard at keeping boundaries, earning respect, and continuing to advocate on Steve's behalf.

Just past noon I hear from Illana. *"WE HAVE A BED!"*

I'm excited but nervous for the trip home, fearing small planes. I'm also worried how Steve will manage the transfer well from a medical perspective. Steve, however, is nothing but excited. He can't stop smiling. This is the next step in Steve's recovery. What a journey so far this has been!

CHAPTER 17

Five weeks later. The trip home

IT HAS BEEN five weeks since Steve's accident, and we are finally leaving VGH. Doctors George I and Robert L come to say goodbye and we hug and take pictures. I am sad to be leaving them. We say our goodbyes to the staff, patients, and even places in the hospital, which have become part of our lives and daily routine over the past five weeks.

While Steve is looking forward to coming home, I am apprehensive, in contrast to how I felt after initially finding out Steve would be airlifted to Vancouver and not Toronto. While Steve sleeps, I sit and reflect on the things that I am grateful for, the medical events we've endured, and the people I have met and come to depend on.

During Steve's hospitalization, I have tried to be as positive as possible. I have made a concerted effort to keep smiling and remain friendly to everyone in the hospital, the doctors, nurses, nursing assistants, desk clerks, cafeteria, and housekeeping staff. Even when feeling scared, lonely, and despondent, I've always tried to radiate a positive aura. It has been one of my coping mechanisms. Maintaining this optimistic and respectful attitude has impacted the care Steve and I received. I am grateful for the small gestures from people who reached out to us, supported us, enhancing our situation during these chaotic and traumatic circumstances. It felt like I had a new extended family taking care of us.

Neither Steve nor I have much to pack, even though we've been here so long. As I leave the hotel saying goodbye to my temporary home, I carry my purse on my shoulder, a carry-on bag, my rolled-up yoga mat and a travel pillow. At the hospital, I pack all of Steve's belongings: two pairs of soccer shorts, two T-shirts, a running jacket, and some toiletries. I place his computer and phone in with my bags. Five weeks and that is the sum of our possessions.

We are now packed and ready to go, but as always with hospital life, we must wait. Steve sleeps in a hospital gown, while I doze next to him. We are told the ambulance will pick us up at two am to take us to the airport, where we will be meeting the medivac.

We are woken up by the night nursing staff. It's dark outside and the hospital is quiet. It feels like we are taking part in a covert activity, exiting from the hospital in the dead of night. I understand that the coordination of Steve's discharge, the availability of a fully fuelled and staffed medivac jet, and the twelve-hour hold on his bed at Sunnybrook is a complicated operation. It has taken much communication and organization to ensure a successful transfer and we are thankful for everyone's efforts.

We leave VGH with our few belongings and a brown paper bag with Steve's medications for the trip. The night nurses have written on the brown paper bag in black marker: *"For Mr. Stephen K. With love from VGH (with a heart drawn on the bag). Have a safe flight home!"*

I get a bit teary when I read this, as the note sums up our stay at VGH. From day one, we have been taken care of, treated with dignity, and loved by this medical family. The nurses are our champions; their frontline work has been critical in shaping Steve's outcome and we are so grateful.

The VGH nurses transfer us to our new medical team for the ambulance ride and flight home. Our umbilical cord to VGH has been cut and our journey home begins. The Latitude Medical Team includes Rob, our nurse, and Jessica, our RT. They are incredibly attentive and well informed, instilling confidence that we will have a safe trip back home.

Rob and Jessica accompany us in the ambulance to the airport and help transfer Steve into the Learjet on a stretcher. He is strapped in tightly and attached to oxygen. His respiration rate, blood pressure and pulse rate are measured and visible on a portable monitor.

Aside from the pilot, there are only three other seats, two for the medical crew and one for an accompanying passenger, me. I sit opposite Steve's stretcher behind Rob and Jessica. The medical staff are extremely focused on Steve's comfort and ability to tolerate the flight. It is an eerie but incredible experience. How often does one get to travel in a Learjet?

We arrive in Toronto at one-thirty pm on Saturday afternoon. An ambulance crew meets us at the airport to take us to Sunnybrook Hospital. Rob and Jessica come with us via ambulance and stay with Steve until he is in his room and signed in, officially completing the transfer to the medical team at Sunnybrook. We are about to see Josh and Gabi, who are on their way to the hospital. Steve and I are so relieved to be back in Toronto and excited to see our children. It has been such a long time.

It is now mid-Saturday afternoon, and Steve is on ward C5, room 69, where he will remain for the next five weeks. The nurses know about Steve and some of my work history here, which helps us settle in smoothly. This is the exact unit that I worked on as a speech-language pathologist about fifteen years earlier. It's surreal to be back, this time as the wife of a patient.

About thirty minutes after we arrive at Sunnybrook, Josh and Gabi arrive. I am unsure how everyone will react and cope. It's an experience that is hard to put into words. They both stand at the door apprehensively, not really knowing what to expect or what to do.

Neither Josh nor Gabi is physically demonstrative or verbal in emotional situations. I hug them both and then stand back. They follow Steve's lead. He has tears in his eyes and gestures for them both to sit on his bed. He takes each of them by the hand and holds them, as if letting go would mean that he would lose them.

Everyone is quiet for a moment. We are all uncomfortable with the silence, so I start the conversation by discussing our Learjet experience. We begin to relax and talk about the kids' trip home, camp, Maddy, and other light topics. We don't cover Steve's medical situation at all. Steve continues to hold onto their hands and neither of them pulls away. It is a calm, tender and quietly emotional reunion. We all sense the relief and are thankful that we are back together again.

Steve wants to go for a walk to show the kids how well he is doing. I know it will be hard for them to see Steve as he is: frail, hesitant, and slow. This is not the strong, healthy dad that they remember. Without hesitation, Josh jumps off the bed, grabs Steve's new walker, and helps him off the bed, knowing just what to do. Gabi follows quietly behind.

If they are shocked by Steve's fragility, neither of them shows any hint of it on their faces. As my family walks slowly down the hallway together, supporting each other, we are on the way to becoming whole again. It is a moment etched in my brain and it gives me comfort that we will be alright.

My parents, Maxine, Phillip, Susie, and Michael all come to spend time with Steve in the afternoon. He is happy to have his family around him. He feels cared for, supported, and safe.

When everything settles, I advocate on Steve's behalf in a "strongly pleasant" manner. I want the medical team here at Sunnybrook to look at the hematoma around his spinal incision. By late afternoon, the general surgery resident comes up to see Steve and examines the leak from his incision site. I request that she call the spine surgeon on call.

Steve is seen by a neurosurgery spine resident, who takes a swab and discusses everything with his team. I tell them everything Dr. Robert L advised me before we left VGH. They agree with his recommendations and are planning to take Steve to surgery so they can open up, clean out, and then drain the hematoma site. They want to consult with the thromboembolic team and get an infectious disease consult prior to surgery. Unfortunately, starting again at another facility takes time to pull everything together.

I'm sure Steve will be in good hands, yet I don't feel quite as confident with his current medical care, as I did under the critical care and spinal teams at VGH. I message Dr. Robert L and we send a series of emails to each other about the process. I verbalize my concerns and jokingly offer to fly him in for the surgery. Clearly, I don't do well with change. He reassures me saying, "I would have preferred to have personally dealt with the hematoma, but that meant staying longer in Vancouver and I know Stephen was desperate to get home. It shouldn't be a big problem to rectify and knowing you, you could probably do the surgery yourself. Keep me posted."

I smile, comforted that he still cares about our well-being even while we are no longer officially patients under his service.

Dr. L advises us that when the surgeons wash out the hematoma, one of two things will happen—either they will close the wound directly or they will put a VAC pump in place. (This vacuum assisted closure uses the controlled negative pressure of a vacuum to promote healing of certain types of wounds.) Either way, I am assured it is a small operation compared to what Steve has been through.

By Monday, many of our friends are messaging us to come visit Steve. He is grateful to have his family and close friends by his side. This makes life seem somewhat more normal and is good for our spirits and souls. I am grateful to be sleeping at home in my own bed, with my children and Maddy around.

We have now been at Sunnybrook for four days and Steve's spine surgery is scheduled for late on the afternoon of Wednesday, August 24. We won't know the extent of the infection until he's in the OR, which will affect the nature of the procedure.

Steve is extremely anxious. He isn't worried about the severity of the infection or the pain or even his recovery. Instead, he is afraid that he is going to die during the surgery. This is a stark contrast from the man whose attitude used to be, "Whatever will happen will happen . . . we have no control over that."

Now that he is reunited with his family, particularly his children, the weight of the situation has set in. He's afraid that he won't be around to be with them. Compared to what he has been through, the risks are far lower, and the recovery should be simpler; nevertheless, he feels extremely vulnerable. He pleads with the anaesthesiologist, "Please don't let anything happen to me. See my amazing family. I want to be with them."

Gabi, Josh, and I look at each other, feeling so badly for Steve. We reassure him that he will make it through and get stronger after this surgery.

We explain that we will be there when he wakes up in recovery. Steve is still insecure, has difficulty sleeping, and has nightmares. We need to protect and encourage him through this next surgery and the ongoing stages of recovery. It's a marked change for our family unit. All of our roles have reversed.

CHAPTER 18

Another spine surgery, counting red cars: August 24 to September 07, Sunnybrook

O N WEDNESDAY, AUGUST 24, Steve undergoes surgery on his spine. The surgeons think he will be in for about three hours, not because the surgery itself is complicated, but because Steve's medical status is complex. He will go to the ICU step-down unit after the OR to monitor his post-surgery recovery. After sitting by his side through so many surgeries, I now trust my instincts. I have a good feeling about this surgery, believing he will have a good outcome. My complicated husband with amazing karma will be okay. He has to be.

Steve comes out of surgery well. They clean the infection, remove the infected tissue, and save the existing metalwork. They insert a drain and a lot of gauze packing to fill up the tissue space until it heals. Gabi and I stay with Steve in recovery, as only two people are allowed in at one time.

When he wakes up from the anaesthetic, Steve talks to us, taking small chips of ice and looking relieved to see our faces. He keeps telling Gabi and me how lovely we are and how much he loves us. By now I am used to the "new and improved" emotional, sweeter, more expressive Steve.

Gabi, however, has yet to discover this new side of her father. She looks at me and asks, "Who is this person?"

We laugh and agree that this sweet, excessively appreciative, highly verbal person feels foreign to us. Though we appreciate his sentiments, a part of us wants our strong and silent husband and father back.

We've always known what an incredible support system we have from our community of friends, family, my clients, Steve's colleagues, and others. But until we return to Toronto, we don't quite appreciate the magnitude of this love. I have never heard of a "meal train," until my friend Robyn organizes this incredible gift for us. Since he is back from camp, Josh is working with Robyn for a humanitarian organization, which delivers poverty alleviation programmes, an organization our family has volunteered with for many years.

The meal train will provide us with meals during this period of time. There is an interactive online calendar and friends are invited to sign up and deliver a meal for us. Robyn and Carolyn become our "food angels" and arrange the process. Josh and Gabi receive the food at home and bring it to the hospital for us to share.

It is such a remarkable gesture and exactly what we need. The meal train takes on a life of its own; forty-eight meals are delivered over the next forty-eight days. So many of our colleagues, clients, family, and friends (even friends of friends!) sign up. We are so incredibly touched and grateful for this practical and thoughtful gift.

The meal train marks the start of a new family tradition, setting up a nightly picnic dinner on Steve's hospital bed. Every night, Josh, Gabi, and I place a plastic tablecloth on his bed and eat with him. We invite the person or family who prepared the meal to join us for dinner. We become known as the party room at Sunnybrook—the family with an overwhelming number of visitors and the best homemade food. Everyone is incredibly thoughtful, providing delicious, healthy meals and including Steve's favourite desserts of ice cream and fresh fruit. We have everything from soups and salads to steak, roasts, chicken, pasta, and sushi.

One of the most special picnics we have is with Linda and her children. She brings sushi and says, "I know this is not homemade brisket or roast chicken . . . you know me."

Honestly, it's more about being with the people who care about us than it is about any specific dish. Steve is thrilled to have Linda and the kids here.

Steve, having progressed in his recovery following his most recent surgery, is no longer confined to eating in bed. He sits in his wheelchair to dine with us. We laugh, share stories, and eat our sushi together. This provides us with a most special memory. We are so grateful for having this extraordinary time all together.

These meals go on into early October. After almost fifty days, the kids and I decide to put an end to the ongoing meal train. It has been the most incredible gift, but we reach a point when we need to get on with our lives, which includes doing our own grocery shopping and cooking. We will always be incredibly grateful and feel fortunate for everyone who stepped up when we needed them.

Steve's post-surgery days are tough for him and all-consuming. He is a little stronger but not as strong as he was before the most recent surgery. His endurance and physical abilities are more limited, and he is in significant pain. He continues to be very fragile medically, despite his progress and even though he looks rather good physically.

Nevertheless, there's another cherished family tradition that we want to maintain. On the last Friday of every month, our family—siblings, cousins, parents, and in-laws—get together for a casual group dinner. This has happened for the past twenty-five years, and it's so important that we rarely miss it. It's an opportunity to catch up with family and enjoy each other's company and conversation. It's something we all look forward to. Unfortunately, Steve's medical crisis meant we could not partake in the July meal.

We decide that we will make every effort to have our August Friday night dinner, all of us together, even if it means setting up at the hospital in a patient/family meeting room. Maxine books a room with Illana's help for six-thirty pm on Friday, August 26, and we order in pizza and bring drinks, fruit, and ice cream. We have put our meal train on hold for the night.

The meal is simple, short, and sweet. We crowd into the tiny, narrow space, which forces us to practically stand or sit on top of each other. Steve is in his wheelchair, attached to an IV and his oxygen, clad in his hospital gown and a Nike jacket to keep warm. Although he is overwhelmed by the experience, he manages to engage in some of the conversation and eat with us. It feels good to do something normal that represents our family's traditions. We celebrate and toast Steve's progress, grateful to be together as an extended family again. This meaningful family activity is about connection, making memories, sharing our lives and being there for each other. It's the tradition we created and one we maintain despite the need to modify and however much effort is involved. I feel this was maybe more for my benefit than Steve's.

It is now Sunday afternoon and Steve is having a relatively good day. He is feeling a little stronger and we even head outside for a short while, the first time since we have been admitted to Sunnybrook. I push Steve in the hospital wheelchair, hoping to get some sun on our faces. Steve has eaten well and has had lots of visitors today.

We have no adventures planned yet, since Steve hasn't been capable of much and we are waiting for his fitted wheelchair to arrive tomorrow. This week will be busy for us. Steve will have his IVC filter removed and a central (pick) line inserted for his IV medications. Once all that is settled, perhaps we'll be able to venture further outside the hospital.

I am still concerned about the impact of Steve's situation on Josh and Gabi, and how it may be affecting their emotional well-being. Josh is working and Gabi starts her final year of high school in early September. They are busy in their routines but make a point of having dinner with Steve almost every night. Although they seem to be coping as well as possible, this can't be easy for them. As any protective mother would be, I worry about how they are adjusting and try to support them in any way I can. I know my children; they tend to internalize their feelings and fears. They get on with what they need to do, but surely this must be affecting them in the long term.

Gabi is dating Jamie, a boy she knows from camp. I am grateful that she has someone who will support her and distract her from our reality. Jamie is coming over to the hospital this evening to meet us for the first time. Meeting one's girlfriend's parents is daunting even under normal circumstances, let alone in a hospital room, and so I imagine he will be quite nervous.

But when Jamie arrives, it's as if we've always known him. He sits on the bed chatting easily with Steve and sharing our picnic dinner. He drives Gabi to the hospital whenever she needs a ride. Through this experience, Jamie becomes part of our family.

Josh's friends Sam and Nina, who are so relaxed with our family, also spend time with us at the hospital, bringing Steve treats and dropping in to check on us, even when Josh isn't there. I realize my kids have a good support system in their group of friends. I am appreciative, as currently a large portion of their lives revolves around the hospital. It is good for them to have some relief and time with their friends and hopefully express their concerns and emotions when they feel comfortable.

While we have a lot of personal support, the administrative side of Steve's ongoing medical issues and all the related paperwork are somewhat taxing for me. We are still dealing with the insurance claims. I am grateful that Maxine and Phillip continue to help us with this, since there is so much correspondence and so many phone calls to make. The personal injury lawyers we are working with contact me. They need all the information about Steve's insurance, medical coverage, and work hours. They need to confirm that he doesn't receive any income from a disability plan, employment insurance benefits, or social assistance. They also need to know what's happened to Steve's motorcycle.

Constable Adam L updates me about Steve's beloved bike, which he released to the local impound. The insurance company is advised of same. Constable L still has Stephen's helmet and SPOT device as well as a CD with pictures taken from the scene. He asks for information on how to ship the items to me. We are appreciative of the constable's help and relieved to get Steve's remaining belongings.

During the week Steve continues to make progress despite some setbacks. The next weekend as he has no surgical procedures or physiotherapy, we have time to relax. His newly rented wheelchair is comfortable and efficient and so Maxine and I decide to take Steve outside the hospital to observe the traffic. This is what we now view as an exciting adventure and change of scenery. This is what we now consider entertainment. How radically our lives have changed!

Here we are, sitting on the sidewalk in front of the hospital, counting red cars as we watch them drive past. This is a family joke, as Steve's mom used to sit outside her retirement home and tell us how many red cars she counted that day. We used to find this quite amusing and now we are doing the same thing. I take a picture of Steve sitting in his wheelchair looking at the road. I send the picture to our family with the caption, "Counting Red Cars." No explanation is needed.

The slow days give us plenty of time to think. Now that I'm back in Toronto, my thoughts turn to my Pilates studio, which has been my career since moving on from speech-language pathology. I miss teaching, working out, and my loyal caring clients. I receive many emails from them, telling me how much they miss the classes; one client even offers to work out with me in the hospital cafeteria.

This makes me smile and know that I am appreciated and needed again in my world, which I so desperately want to be a part of again. These emails matter so much, as I feel like I am losing the person I was.

On September 6, I receive an email from the marketing and communications officer at VGH, asking if we wish to share our experience and story for their annual newsletter. After discussing with Steve, I reply that we would be happy to participate. I emphasize that the care was exemplary and thank her for their interest in our experience.

The following afternoon, we conduct the interview from Steve's hospital bed, setting my cell phone on speaker mode. Steve tells his story, at least what he remembers, and for as long as he's able to concentrate. I fill in the gaps and relate our experience. I try hard not to speak for Steve, as I have been doing for the past six weeks, to allow his voice and thoughts to be heard. But it's difficult, as our stories are entwined.

CHAPTER 19

September 09

I CONTINUE TO SPEND every day and evening with Steve, leaving the hospital around ten pm every night. My routine hasn't changed much since Vancouver, but at least I have my family to support and spend time with Steve. I have a little more time for myself and am in the comforts of my own home. Fortunately, the hospital is a short drive from our home.

Friday September 9 is my father's birthday and a difficult day for Steve. This past week has been particularly tough for him. It is now eight weeks since this roller coaster journey began and he has now developed fluid in his right lung, is short of breath, and is unable to walk much. He is scheduled to have a small surgical procedure tonight to drain the fluid.

Another surgery. It's hard to believe. I hope he will progress without any more setbacks. I am always hopeful, despite every setback, despite the odds. He has come so far, yet for every two steps forward he seems to take one step back. It reminds me that recovery is not necessarily a linear process.

Steve's anxiety increases when becomes aware that he will need a chest tube to remove the fluid from his lung. A fourth-year medical student and her supervising physician are not sensitive to Steve's fragile medical and emotional needs, and before getting consent, they list the possible risks and complications, some of which Steve has already experienced.

The panic on Steve's face shows how traumatized he is. I understand that it's standard protocol to advise patients of all risks prior to a procedure, but it's detrimental for Steve, who has endured many of the low-risk complications that are listed prior to surgery.

I am so concerned and overly protective of Steve that when the medical student begins describing all the risks, I interrupt her, assertively direct the medical team out of the room, and insist they explain things to me instead. I advise them that I'll explain the risks to Steve so that he can sign the consent.

I explain Steve's emotional fragility and suggest that, in the future, when reading a patient's chart, the full medical history, including understanding the mental health impacts of trauma should be considered prior to presenting an onslaught of medical information. In Steve's case, sharing all this information may be detrimental and approaching the family first may be more appropriate.

Even though Steve is likely cognitively competent at this point, he is not emotionally stable enough to deal with the implications. Perhaps I am too harsh on the doctors, expecting too much and overlooking pre-surgery protocol; however, at this point, Steve's physical and emotional well-being remains my priority. When I get my composure back and reflect on what was said, I hope I did not chase away this young medical student. The team comes back to apologize for causing Steve any further stress. The medical student is nowhere to be seen.

Still, Steve remains determined to take on his challenges. He is now designated NPO (nothing per oral) and is back on an IV to administer hydration and medication. He is waiting for a chest tube to be inserted. It is a long day and night of waiting. I finally leave the hospital around eleven pm, still without any indication of the time of his surgery.

I remain awake throughout the night, anxiously wondering how Steve is doing. I call the nursing unit at three am and again at seven, only to be told that Steve is still waiting (asleep but waiting). Finally, at eight-thirty am, he is taken to the OR for the chest tube to be inserted.

A chest tube will help drain air, blood, or infection from the space between the lungs and chest wall (pleural space) and is inserted through the side of the body between the ribs. This is a particularly painful procedure. Steve experiences excruciating pain for the next ten hours. He describes the pain as worse than when he was lying on the ground waiting for help in Yukon.

Despite numerous doctors called to deal with Steve's pain, he remains in agony. He is suffering and it breaks my heart not being able to help him.

It is a bad day all round—Steve in such anguish and Gabi homesick, stressed, and overwhelmed. I am so torn. Yet again, I need to be in two places at once. Josh, Maxine, and my parents stay with Steve, and I go home to be with Gabi.

Finally, in the evening, after receiving an effective cocktail of pain medications, Steve seems to be coping. He's able to sit up in bed and chat with us. Gabi is feeling better too, and we all picnic on Steve's bed, relieved that this difficult day is behind us. Once again, we are drained and exhausted.

Steve continues to have PTSD. Despite the length of time, he has been in hospital, he remains anxious and afraid of his medical condition and the most basic treatments. He has developed a fear of having his IV changed or blood taken because his veins have collapsed, and it is difficult for the nurses to do either. Frequently, his nurses are unsuccessful at trying to draw blood, which leads to constant prodding. This creates marked anxiety in Steve. He becomes so stressed that every time I have to hold his hand and talk him through the procedure.

It is hard to see him panic over such a relatively small procedure, after all the major surgeries and invasive treatments he has experienced. After a few attempts, the unit nurses usually resort to summoning the specialized IV nurse to find a vein and insert the needle to draw blood or replace his IV. Although still anxious, he seems to have more confidence when one of the IV nurses does it.

It is now Tuesday, September 13 and Steve is feeling determined and spirited again. He is managing his pain with pain medications. Despite his chest tube appendage, he walks the long hallway using a high-wheeled walker. Together, we make it to the elevator and down to the hospital lobby. It is a huge distance and a great accomplishment for him, and we celebrate with "drinks." When we make it back upstairs, he even walks a lap around the unit unaided. When his pain is managed, his progress is amazing. He can't wait for the limiting chest tube to be removed.

Our friends continue to be supportive, though it comes more naturally for some than others. I find that some people are unsure how to help us, when to give us space, and when to visit. They struggle knowing what to say and what not to say. It's a time when people want to reach out, but it's also a time when people fear saying or doing the wrong thing.

Looking back, I just needed to know that we could depend on people to come through for us when they said they would or even just show that they cared. I wanted our friends to be there, to talk normally about daily, mundane things, to engage Steve, to make him laugh, to lift his spirits, and to bring the outside world in. I wanted our friends to remind us that we were cared for and that our lives once out of the hospital would still be enriched, even if different.

After five weeks on the trauma ward C5 in Sunnybrook, we again make new friends, share experiences, support one another, and speak frankly about our family members, ups and downs. There is the wife whose husband has fallen off a ladder and has a brain injury and parents whose teenage son was crushed by a construction vehicle. Each patient and each family we meet shapes our own journey.

The most traumatic situation that I encounter involves the woman in the room next to Steve's. Two of her four young daughters aged eight and twelve years old had been killed by a drunk driver. Her two older daughters as well as herself survived the crash.

I see and chat with her family in the hallway. They share with me the story and how she and her other daughters are recovering. I feel completely devastated for them.

On the day of the funerals of both her daughters, the family asks me to come and meet the mother and see the collage of pictures they have created to display at the funerals.

Anxiety washes over me as I walk into the room. I am at a loss for words and have no idea what to say. I fumble through the entire conversation, talking to the mother, who will soon go to her daughters' funerals by ambulance. I try holding back my tears and take this mother's hand and hold it. I can't imagine the intense pain she must be feeling.

I know she must be numb from shock and medication, but she still has the generosity of spirit to ask me how Steve is doing. She tells me she is praying for him. I have no idea how to respond to this and so I gently smile, tears pooling in my eyes. I have often wondered how she has coped with her life after this devastating loss to her family, but due to the transient nature of hospital wards, I'll likely never know.

Despite the stress and Steve's ongoing medical issues, we try to see the humour in our situation and laugh when we can. His sense of dignity and privacy have been left at the hospital entrance, despite our best efforts. Steve has a small en suite bathroom attached to his room at Sunnybrook. He is still not fully independent with his self-care tasks: body washing, hair washing, shaving, etc.

He perches on a special seat in the bath while I shower him with a handheld spray attachment. The water is either too cold or sprays every-where, inevitably leaving both of us freezing and soaked. We laugh at the wet mess. After the shower, he stands holding onto the basin for support while I dry and cream his body. His skin is so grey and flaky, and all his muscles having atrophied.

In the early period of his hospitalization, I used to think Steve had become an old man, looking ninety years old. I've watched him "age back-wards" over the following weeks, starting to show glimpses of his "younger" self. I look at him and say, "You are definitely Benjamin Button."

Perhaps today I am more fatigued, or maybe I have lost my sensitivity, or maybe we just need a good laugh. I look at him standing naked holding onto the basin and say, "Steve, you have the butt of an eighty-year-old. It's no longer firm and strong. It's sagging down to the floor and you have no meat or muscle left!"

We both start to laugh, tears rolling down our faces. Moments like these are good stress relievers.

By Wednesday, September 14, Steve is doing much better. The chest tube comes out, which leaves him with less pain and more mobility. He is walking independently and even relearning how to climb a flight of stairs. The plan is that any day now he will go to a rehabilitation hospital for a short stay. It's hard to believe how far he has come in such a short time. Clearly there is no holding him back.

CHAPTER 20

Two months later / onto rehab (September 15)

WHEN I ARRIVE at the hospital on Thursday morning, Steve's nurse tells me that he will be transferred to St. John's Rehab tomorrow. This is an amazing milestone. Two months after the accident, he is finished with acute hospitalization and ready for rehabilitation. Weekends aren't the best time for a transfer because staffing is minimal, but we are truly grateful to be moving forward.

This period of rehabilitation and preparation for coming home is important for all of us. I am not quite ready to bear the full responsibility of Steve's medical care, pain management, and limited mobility. The thought of such responsibility is quite daunting after everything we've been through. And so a short stay in rehab is exactly what we all need, some time to evolve into our new life post-accident and post-immediate recovery.

Friday at noon, Steve is taken to St. John's Rehab by ambulance. We are both anxious, as although it is a step forward, it is yet another unfamiliar medical environment. Following the ambulance in my car, my feelings are that this will not be an easy transition. Like Steve's overall hospitalization, his rehabilitation experience proves to be complicated.

And then Steve's in rehabilitation for less than one day when he is taken back to Sunnybrook Hospital. It is Saturday and true to form, there is never a dull moment in Steve's journey. The cause of Steve's re-hospitalization is a blocked central line. The central line delivers his medication, particularly the antibiotic for his spine infection. Steve messages me early in the morning to update me on this newest complication and is then taken by ambulance to back Sunnybrook.

Josh, Susie, Maxine, and I meet Steve in Sunnybrook's emergency room. They have unblocked the central line and he is cleared to go back to rehab. We sit for hours in the ER waiting for the ambulance to take Steve back. We know we need to be patient, as the paramedics are busy responding to emergent calls. So, we spend most of his first day in rehab in the ER. It means Steve is missing his therapy for the day. We hope for better things tomorrow.

One issue is solved before the next crisis arrives. Steve must adjust from living in a quiet private room in both VGH and Sunnybrook (we were lucky; we realize that is a luxury), to a semi-private room at St. John's with another patient.

Since the accident, Steve is destined to connect with truckers. Jeff, his friendly new roommate, drives a transport rig. Jeff was in a traumatic accident during which his truck caught fire and his legs are severely burned. The impact of having Jeff as Steve's roommate is significant. Burn patients require considerable nursing care, and the treatment is often painful. Jeff needs to have his burns debrided, as well as receive skin grafts. His dressings are changed at least twice a day. Even though the curtains are drawn, listening to Jeff's painful cries causes Steve to panic, adding to his severe anxiety. Although he wants to empathize with Jeff, he is fearful of these medical treatments. In order to protect Steve, we come up with a plan for the nurses to wheel Steve into the common sitting area every time Jeff has his dressing changed. This seems to help Steve manage his day and allows him and Jeff to spend time together between the treatments.

In rehab, Steve is finally able to use his phone and computer independently. He emails or texts me each morning to say hello or to let me know what he needs before I come in. We have worked so hard to get Steve to where he is, having sustained so many setbacks. When Steve calls me concerned that his current nurse is taking shortcuts and not using sterile techniques and instruments to change his dressing, I am so distressed. We can't afford another infection. Proper measures involve meticulous hand washing, use of a sterile field, sterile gloves for applying a sterile dressing and sterile instruments.

As soon as I arrive at the hospital later that morning, I verbalise my concern to the nurse in charge. I try to be respectful and choose my words carefully, but I won't accept anything less than the best care. I remain a force to be reckoned with when it comes to Steve's medical issues. Throughout his hospitalization I have remained vigilant, not missing a thing, or allowing him to be put under any unnecessary risk or preventable complication. I am relieved when Steve emails me advising that the nurse is now following the correct sterile procedures.

Sunday starts off as a pleasant and uneventful day, and I am glad to see Steve feeling optimistic and energetic. Steve has physiotherapy and we enjoy relaxing with family and friends outside in the garden. After the visitors leave, Steve and I sit quietly on his bed. We talk about his progress and the fact that after all this time he is coming home in a few days. He is excited and feeling confident, ready for this next phase. Although I am apprehensive and feeling somewhat insecure, I don't let on.

Later, we will have dinner with Josh and Gabi in the hospital's dining room, as we no longer picnic on Steve's bed. Josh and I still bring in the home cooked meals prepared by family and friends as part of the ongoing meal train. I am looking forward to our family eating together, preparing Steve for bed, and then heading home for the night with Josh and Gabi.

Unfortunately, life has other plans in store. I shouldn't be surprised. Nothing so far has been simple or smooth. Ahead of us is yet another trip to the emergency room—the second time in two days.

It is late afternoon and we're chatting on Steve's bed. He has set the alarm on his watch to beep every hour to remind him to do the deep breathing exercises for his lungs. He has been doing this for two weeks and still needs the reminder. I notice that although his alarm goes off repeatedly, he does not react. He tells me he doesn't hear it.

I set the alarm to go off again to test Steve's hearing. He then casually mentions that a nurse commented earlier in the day that he didn't notice his alarm. He doesn't make the connection that he may not be hearing certain sounds. Immediately, I become concerned.

There's a rare but potential side effect of the IV Vancomycin—profound hearing loss. Vancomycin is a potent antibiotic. I ask Steve if he's noticed whether his hearing has recently deteriorated. He says now that I mention it, it has been difficult to hear in noisy situations and that he has had some ringing in his ears. Ototoxicity, tinnitus, or bilateral sensorineural hearing loss can occur in association with elevated Vancomycin serum concentrations, resulting in irreversible hearing loss.

When Steve was prescribed this antibiotic, there was a slight risk; however, the infectious disease team felt that Vancomycin would be the best antibiotic to treat his spinal infection. After everything he has been through, to lose his hearing now would be devastating and unfair.

My adrenaline races and I speak to the nurses at the nursing station, explaining this latest development, and telling them we need to get him back to Sunnybrook urgently. Steve needs to see the infectious disease team, so he can be taken off the IV Vancomycin and have it replaced with another antibiotic.

It is Sunday evening, and so everything moves at a slow pace. I ask the nurse to contact the doctor on call to release Steve to go back to Sunnybrook. Steve's hearing is dependent on getting him back to the ER right away. I feel a bit panicked because I'm unsure how extensive the effects of the ototoxicity (poison) might be on his hearing. Perhaps I am again overreacting to what I think is an urgent situation, but I'm not willing to take any chances.

We wait for the ambulance to pick him up. As you can imagine, calling the paramedics for a potential hearing loss is not an urgent priority compared to the other calls they receive. I know we will be waiting for a few hours, so I decide that I am going to drive Steve in my car to the hospital and not waste another minute. I tell the staff of my decision. They are concerned for Steve's safety and their liability, but I have made up my mind.

The nurses help me get Steve into my car, which is not an easy feat. The seat in my SUV is high and he needs a lot of support to climb in. We fold his wheelchair and put it in the trunk.

Once we are driving, Steve is quite excited to be outside the hospital. I think for him, this is another adventure. He has not been in a car for over two months; this is another new sensation and experience. He is enthralled with the trees, the road, the houses, and the traffic.

It is like he is seeing everything for the first time. I am taken aback by how novel and interesting this drive is for him. It shows how much he has been deprived of and how appreciative he is for things that the rest of us take for granted.

We arrive at the hospital emergency entrance and get Steve into the wheelchair. He waits while I park, and then we head into the waiting area. Some of the staff greet us with a smile, noting that we are back again so soon. Clearly, we are having a hard time leaving Sunnybrook.

I have called our family, and they all meet us at the ER. Steve is now quite well known by the many specialists at Sunnybrook, and we don't have to wait long for the infectious disease team. He is taken off the IV Vancomycin and is given Doxycycline, now taken orally. This means that he no longer needs the central line, which ironically was the reason for our visit to emergency yesterday. We could have saved a trip!

We are happy to get rid of the central line, the Vancomycin and return to St. John's. Josh and I drive Steve back to rehab later that night. To this day, Steve still presents with a mild high-frequency sensorineural hearing loss and some tinnitus. I have subsequently read that patients with renal failure, like Steve, are more susceptible to Vancomycin- and Erythromycin-induced hearing loss. Still, it could have been much worse.

By Monday, September 19, Steve is having a great day. He has no trips or adventures, only his therapies, time on the stationary reclining bike and dinner together as a family. We leave Steve at about nine pm hoping to have an early night after the intense and hectic weekend.

When we arrive home, Josh lets Maddy out into the backyard as we usually do. About ten minutes later, I call her back inside. She is nowhere to be found, despite the gates being closed and latched. The only place she has ever gone on her own is the small park across the road from our house, but she is not there. We are panicked and search for over two hours in the rain, by car and by foot. It is now midnight, and we still haven't found Maddy.

We can't explain her disappearance, the first time in the seven years she has been with us. We are all distraught.

How are we going to tell Steve that his dog is gone? He can't wait to come home, and one of the main reasons is to see Maddy. As if the weekend, with all of Steve's medical crises, wasn't bad enough, now our beautiful, sweet dog is missing, and we can't find her. We are anxious. Although Josh calmly reassures us that we will find Maddy, Gabi and I need an Ativan to sleep.

The next morning, I am woken up by the doorbell at six am. Our neighbour, while looking out his front window, saw a woman walking Maddy along with her own dog. He rushed out to get her. The woman said she found Maddy on our street. Gabi and I start to cry from relief and Josh hugs her. To this day, we have never worked out how she disappeared from our enclosed backyard or how she came home perfectly clean and dry, despite the rainstorm the previous night. It was just another crisis we had to deal with that somehow worked out. This seemed to be a pattern in our lives during this time, crisis after crisis, but somehow pulling through.

The rest of the week is uneventful. On Wednesday afternoon, Steve will be coming home for a few hours to have an early dinner with us. He hasn't been home for over two and a half months since the day he embarked on his "Alaska or Bust" journey.

Steve's first-time home is an interesting experience, nothing like we predict. He has an afternoon and evening pass from the rehab facility. After completing his therapy for the day, we arrive home by five-thirty pm. He says he is excited to be coming home, but I sense some apprehension. Steve feels safe in his hospital environment and any change makes him insecure.

So even though he is excited to come home permanently, it is a period of adjustment. It is tiring for him to walk up the stairs to the front door, while simultaneously holding onto Josh and the railing. He concentrates on each step as he walks slowly with the walker into our kitchen and sits down on a chair.

Even Maddy is not quite her normal energetic self. We expect her to jump up to greet Steve, but she senses his need to be protected and is quite docile. She walks slowly by his side as if to say, "I've got you."

We all try hard to make his return home exciting, special, and comfortable; however, it is quite overwhelming for him, both emotionally and physically, and somewhat uneasy for all of us. We need to learn how to adjust to his presence here, even for this short period. A vastly different Steve is home, someone who is psychologically and physically injured.

We see how much he needs his structure and routine; this outing has disrupted his daily schedule. It requires so much endurance, concentration, and physical effort for him to enjoy his time at home. We want to make it work for him, for us.

However, this early stilted dinner is a far cry from the natural chatty chaos that usually ensues when we eat together. Maddy lies quietly at Steve's feet, as if she's taking care of him. We sit for a while quietly eating at the kitchen table, sensitive to Steve's limited coping ability.

Then, about an hour after being at home, Steve asks if we can take him back to the rehab facility. He wants to lie down on "his" bed. The three of us are all taken aback by his request. We thought he would have begged to stay home and sleep here.

In fact, I had already thought about how to encourage him when it was time to return. I had prepared a script in my head, forming the perfectly supportive words to use when explaining the need to go back to the rehab facility for the night. It is a conversation that we obviously don't need to have.

Nevertheless, despite how draining this brief visit home is for Steve, it somehow must have motivated and energized him. The next day, September 22, he sends an email to everyone on his list:

> "If everything goes according to plan, I'm going to be released from rehab on Saturday and will be going home. After nearly eleven weeks in various hospitals, I can't wait to be home with my family. Thanks to everyone for their well wishes and caring. It certainly helped me get through some difficult times.
> —Steve.

After everything we've gone through, it really is quite remarkable that he'll be home in a few days. If I've learned anything from this experience, it's that life and everything in it—events, behaviours, and even emotions—are unpredictable.

Marcus, the CEO of Brita, the water filter company in Germany where Steve works, replies to Steve's email.

Marcus states, *"There is nothing more important than recovering and get(ting) healthy again."* He ends his note by stating they will wait for Steve as long as is necessary.

This is a testament to the hard work and many years Steve put in at Brita prior to his accident and how much they value him at the company. It allows us to relax and focus on Steve's recovery while knowing his job is waiting.

The rest of Steve's stay in rehab is uneventful and short-lived, only lasting four more days. Steve attends his physical and occupational therapy sessions every morning in the gym and the therapy room. He works on his strength, balance, and endurance. He uses the stationary bike, climbs stairs, and lifts weights. He works on increasing his walking tolerances.

His goal is to become as functional as possible prior to discharge home. The afternoons are spent sleeping and socializing with family and friends. The evenings are the same picnic dinners, but he is now strong enough to eat them in the hospital cafeteria.

On Friday morning, I get a call from Steve saying he wants to come home a day earlier than scheduled. He is now motivated and determined to escape from institutions and start his newly adjusted life at home. Steve really does everything fast. A couple of days ago the hospital gave him security, and now he wants out. He is ready to tackle the reality of life at home. But I'm anxious about shouldering the full responsibility of Steve's care at home.

It's quite an undertaking to get him discharged a day early, involving arranging his medical scripts, coordinating home nursing, and ensuring we have the necessary supplies. But Steve had made up his mind and nothing will deter him and so we do what we can and make it happen.

CHAPTER 21

Eleven weeks later / home / September 23 to January 2012

FINALLY, THE TIME has come. Steve has been discharged and he couldn't be happier. There were many points when we thought this day would never arrive. I send out an update to my group:

It is Friday, September 23rd and Steve is now home, discharging himself a day earlier than planned, but that is typical of Steve, always ahead of the game. He is now cozy, sleeping in his own bed, for the first time since July 1st. So, begins the next stage of his journey, working towards strengthening, increasing endurance, becoming independent and enjoying life. We are all together at home at last.

After everything we've been through, I can't quite believe Steve is home. We have prescriptions to fill, medications to administer, nursing to coordinate, and therapies to manage.

His wheelchair is parked in the garage where his motorcycle used to be, a symbolic change of wheels. But we hardly use it at all because Steve is determined to walk as much as he can. We keep his walker on the main level of the house. He has been working on stair climbing in therapy and with our support and much effort on his part, he is able to manage the stairs up to the bedroom level of the house.

Somehow, we sort everything out. We all work together to support Steve: Josh, Gabi, family, friends, and me. On his first night home, he takes his medications and has a great sleep. This is a good sign, but still, I lie in bed awake, anxiously watching him.

We slowly ease into our new lives with Steve back home. He has many follow-up appointments at Sunnybrook Hospital. It seems as if we are there at least twice a week. He is followed by the thromboembolism clinic weekly to check on his PT-INR levels. As well, the trauma surgeon, spine surgeon, infectious disease physicians, cardiac surgeon, and internists continue to monitor him for various concerns.

A home care nurse initially comes twice a day to change his spine wound dressings. I have watched and helped the nurses at Sunnybrook and at St John's Rehab, so when the nurse feels it necessary to only come every second and then third day, I change Steve's dressings in between. I am now confident and experienced in following the sterile techniques and have all the necessary instruments.

I also give Steve his blood thinner injections twice a day into his stomach. He gets markedly anxious before these injections, as he feels a burning pain for about thirty seconds afterwards. I must verbally prepare him and ease him into having the injection while he does his deep breathing exercises to relax.

Steve is still emotionally fragile and at times afraid. However, I feel that since he is home, motivated by his progress and feeling more secure, his PTSD seems to be lifting. He is less distressed when talking about his medical issues and the accident, his nightmares and flashbacks seem to have reduced, he is more interested in life around him, he is engaged in our daily activities, he appears less detached, and he is developing a more positive outlook on his life moving forward. This is a huge relief for me.

Physically he is improving by the day. There are times when Steve walks and exerts himself too much and then suffers intense back pain. He takes Percocet, a strong painkiller, when needed. He sleeps a lot during his recovery, napping at least twice a day.

We realize over time that Steve not only has weakness of his right leg but also a dropped right shoulder and mild right facial weakness. We feel that this is likely from a mild stroke which may have occurred during the period when Steve was critically ill. These issues were likely overlooked, as he was far too sick for his treatment team to notice.

We receive medical supplies and professional services at home through homecare. The occupational therapist and physiotherapist come to our house until Steve can be treated in their clinics as an outpatient.

William, our friend and a skilled personal trainer, works out with Steve twice a week. Our lives are busy! Rehabbing Steve and ensuring his medical stability is a full-time job. Josh walks with Steve, helps with his therapies, and drives him to many of his appointments. I am so grateful to Josh and Gabi for coming through for their dad during this period. They should be out socializing and enjoying their lives as young adults, yet Steve remains their priority.

Josh is our backbone and is always in the right place when we need him. Besides me, he becomes Steve's main source of support and Steve relies on him for everything. They bond over this experience and Josh comes through for Steve in the most immeasurable way.

Gabi is exceptional throughout our experience. Her ability to stay focused, to get done what needs to be done, is crucial. She keeps me grounded and in touch with our lives. She loves and nurtures Steve which he needs. Gabi and I laugh and cry together, working our way through this.

At the end of September, we hear back from VGH and the UBC Hospital Foundation about Steve's story. Steve's medical treatment at VGH is being featured in their community report. A two-page insert makes it to the *Vancouver Sun* as the lead story.

It is now time for me to get back to my own life and work. I am finally ready, mentally and physically, to start teaching Pilates again. Steve is now fairly independent at home and we are organized in terms of his appointments and therapies. On October 3, I email my clients to let them know I will start classes again on October 11.

The responses I receive are reinforcing. Fitness is a fickle industry and I have been concerned that people would have moved on. I am relieved and grateful that most of my clients have waited over three months to come back and work out with me. It is great to have these loyal and appreciative people in my life and I am thankful for their support and kindness.

One of my clients writes back: *"You are back in the saddle and in your workout leggings again."*

It's amazing how therapeutic exercise is for the body, mind, and soul. It helps me move on and begin to heal from the past traumatic few months.

It is now four months after his accident. Our lives go on, though we are changed forever. We learn to adjust and accept what lies ahead. We celebrate Steve's fifty-fifth birthday with a big party at home. The invitations read, *"It's 11/11/11, he's 55 and alive."*

In December, we go on a family vacation to a resort in the Dominican Republic. Even though Steve's medical history prevents him from getting medical travel insurance, we decide to take the chance that he will be "healthy enough" on our trip. Normally I would be hesitant to go under these circumstances, but after our wild experience with Steve having "nine lives," I throw caution to the wind. It is a regrouping for our family of four and we spend a relaxed and pleasant week together.

In early January, Steve sends an email to the company from whom he'd purchased the SPOT GPS tracker, with the *Vancouver Sun* article attached. His wants to send a testimonial about his rescue, so that the value of the SPOT is reinforced. We are incredibly grateful that Steve purchased this GPS tracker, which enabled him to send out an emergency alert from such a remote location and be rescued.

Steve's story is published online as a testimonial. It highlights how the SPOT tracker works in a critical situation, notifying emergency services of the remote GPS location, even when there is no cellular or radio reception. We hope Steve's testimonial will help save more lives.

More publications are drawn to our story. Steve has a huge supporter in our friend Linda, the editor-in-chief of *More Magazine* Canada. In the December 2011/January 2012, she writes a piece called, "Is Health the New Wealth?"

Linda refers to good health as the new luxury item, mentioning her own health issues: a blood disorder following chemotherapy treatment.

She writes about our attitudes when sick and how illness reminds us that life is a precious gift. She explains that over time that positive attitude and sense of gratitude subside and are replaced by the "mundane minutiae that occupy us every day."

Linda has a wonderful way with language, with the skill to blend wit, sincerity, humour, and gravity. She ends her column with the following:

> *If this all sounds too bah humbug, take note: This holiday season, I've decided to quiet the cynic in me. My attitude of gratitude has been reawakened by a friend, who recently spent 10 weeks in hospital. After a horrific motorcycle accident in the Yukon last summer, Stephen was given less than five percent chance to live. Today, the look on his face as he describes the bliss and wonder he feels every time he experiences a new "first"—his first step, his first shower—says it all. So please allow me, in all sincerity, to wish you a truly luxurious holiday.*

Linda follows this column with an online note:

> ***Warning: A shameless plea for money:*** *In my Letter from Linda column this issue, I wrote about the horrific motorcycle accident of my friend Steve. Some of you have asked how he is doing. Well, he is surviving and, we hope, on his way to thriving. In fact, today he flew to Chicago . . . on a business trip! What saved him—the GPS locator that landed miraculously within reach of his hand? The truck driver who found him on a remote road in the Yukon? Or the extracorporeal membrane oxygenation (ECMO) machine that kept his heart and lungs functioning after spinal fracture, a pulmonary embolism, multiple-organ failure and cardiac arrest?*
>
> *I like to think it was sheer will, for which Steve is known. But the miracle of modern medicine (a cliché if I ever heard one, but it's apt) certainly played a huge role. No wonder, then, when he celebrated his birthday recently, in lieu of gifts Steve asked for donations to his home away from home, Vancouver General Hospital (worldclasshealthcare.ca).*
> —*Linda L, Editor-in-Chief linda@more.ca*

The year 2012 is another tough period for us. My dad is diagnosed with malignant melanoma (skin cancer) requiring surgery and radiation treatment. Linda is diagnosed with leukemia (AML) and faces a year of challenging treatments and hospitalizations. We continue to work on Steve's recovery, as well as support my dad and Linda during their battles with cancer. It is agonizing to see both Linda and my dad endure these diseases. Linda is determined to take on every challenge and demonstrate "sheer will," the term she used to describe Steve.

CHAPTER 22

Fifteen months following his accident. Life goes on

IT HAS NOW been one year and three months since Steve's accident. Life is almost back to the hectic pace that we once knew before. Steve is working full time, travelling and now responsible for the financial and operations of two companies. He is still undergoing physiotherapy and works out when he can, as it is essential to improve on and maintain the strength of his back and leg muscles.

He has upgraded his wheelchair and downgraded his BMW endurance motorcycle for a BMW bicycle. It's amazing that he wants to ride/cycle again, as a year ago he felt he would never get back on a two wheeler. Steve rides his bicycle and goes for long walks with brief spurts of slow-paced running, tending to rapidly become short of breath.

We go on canoe trips and hikes with friends. On one canoe trip, Steve passes out from overexerting himself. Thank goodness for good friends and Gatorade! Even with changes after the accident, it's never dull living with Steve.

He is now working in Vancouver for almost a week every month and I am planning a few days of vacation to coincide with his work there. I haven't been back to Vancouver since we left that night on a Learjet. We feel it's now time to visit VGH and the staff who took such incredible care of us. I email Dr. George I in late September to plan a time for all of us to meet.

It is October 18, 2012, and Steve and I are back together in Vancouver, this time under very different circumstances. Steve has been in Vancouver for a few weeks working, and I fly in from Los Angeles, after taking a course and spending some time with old school friends. Although Steve has been working in Vancouver for a while, he waits for me to come before returning to VGH.

We plan to visit the staff at VGH and show Steve the units of the hospital where he spent five very tough weeks. There is much he doesn't remember. I have been in contact with some of the staff to let them know we are coming. I have to say I am feeling quite nervous, not knowing how I will react after all this time. Steve is in high spirits, looking forward to the experience.

The day is overcast, with rain predicted. We catch a cab from the hotel, and as we drive up the hill to the hospital, I point out to Steve the different landmarks that I have become so familiar with. We walk into the entrance of VGH and my reaction catches me off guard. My heart is racing, and I am apprehensive and teary.

It's interesting that I am so emotional, as I rarely cried during the whole VGH experience. I must have been protecting myself but now those defences are down. I should know how to get down to the ICU; after all, I did so countless times last year. But my internal GPS isn't connecting and shockingly we must ask for directions.

Steve is both curious and excited. It is time for him to see where he spent so much time and meet the people who saved his life. We walk into the maze of the ICU and it feels like a lifetime ago that we were here. We meet with the brilliant, compassionate, and modest Dr. George I. As amazing as all the physicians and staff were, I believe that our experience and journey through the ICU and in VGH were much more exceptional because of Dr. I.

We walk into his office and are greeted by a huge, warm smile and hug. It has been well over a year since we left VGH, and our connection is just as strong as when Steve had been under his care. We spend the next forty-five minutes sharing our experiences since we left VGH, laughing at funny moments and asking about the staff.

I'm no longer apprehensive or weepy, just happy to be back. I can't wait for all the staff to see how amazingly Steve has recovered. Dr. I reminds me of our intense negotiations that awful evening, regarding whether and how to save Steve. He tells us that Steve was as critical as one could be. He says they took a "long shot" in treating him with ECMO, as at the time it was not possible to anticipate his survival and certainly not his miraculous outcome.

Dr. I takes us on a tour of the ICU, and he pages some of the doctors who had treated or knew of Steve to come and meet with us. It feels surreal but exciting to meet up with some of the doctors, nurses, RTs and, specifically, Dr. Morad H, who took over Steve's care when Dr. I went off his clinical rotation. He is the kindest gentleman of a physician, with a shy smile, who showed the utmost concern for our well-being. In addition to caring for Steve, I remember him asking me if I was eating, if I was okay at the hotel, and if I was managing.

I remember an encounter with Dr. H who told me that Steve's story is worthy of a movie. With his reserved smile, he asked me who would play Steve. Without hesitation I answered Ewan McGregor since they drove the same BMW endurance motorbike, and both enjoyed long-distance motorcycle adventures.

These memories all flood back, as I see him walking down the ICU hallway towards us. I give him the biggest hug, and despite him appearing slightly uncomfortable, his face lights up and he tells me how happy he is to see us. It's clear that he can't believe how well Steve looks. He smiles as he says that he's been keeping an eye out for the movie.

Each person we see can't get over how incredibly well Steve has done. They are touched by the fact that we have come back to visit and that Steve's outcome has been remarkable, way beyond expectations. They express that seeing someone who was so critically ill walk back into the ICU looking so good validates how worthwhile their work is. They rarely get to see how an ICU patient fares after recovery, and Steve exemplifies the best outcome they could ever have imagined.

We go to the spinal step-down unit, the ward where Steve spent so much time. Unfortunately, we don't get to see Dr. Robert L, as he is now working in a hospital in London, England. The nurses and nurse aides are amazed when Steve walks back into the area. The last time he was here, he was gaunt, anxious, and in a wheelchair, just starting to learn how to walk again. This is a healthy, handsome, well-dressed man who walks independently. Just looking at Steve today, one could never believe what he has been through.

We meet with Hillary, his physiotherapist, who was the first person to give Steve the motivation to move forward. Steve tells Hillary that the first time he was able to stand with her support, using the parallel bars, he knew that he would conquer everything. We see his speech-language pathologist, who gushes about how incredible he looks. With the spinal unit coordinator, we reminisce about how stressful the medivac transfer to Toronto was. She says how grateful she is that we have come back to visit and that Steve's recovery is remarkable.

I realize what a necessary experience returning to VGH is for Steve and me, helping to obtain closure for such a traumatic period in our lives. Steve tells me that he feels satisfaction being back at VGH as a healthier, stronger, independent version of himself, the person he has known he was. Further, meeting the staff and seeing the physical environment is helping fill in some of his memory gaps.

We also visit our spinal ward friends Shannon, his wife, and their twin babies in their home. The two men now stand upright, without walkers, arms around each other and a smile on their faces. This beautiful moment belies what they both endured to get to this day.

By October 2012, Lance Armstrong's reputation is in tatters. The victories that made him a cycling legend have been wiped away, and he loses his credibility and his sponsors. He is stripped of his seven Tour de France titles and later confesses to taking performance-enhancing drugs. Steve is shaken by the fall of an athlete who had become a global sporting icon. Lance Armstrong had always been an inspiration for Steve. In the past, he had followed all the Tour de France races; once, we arranged to be at the finish line in Barcelona, and it was a highlight of the trip for Steve.

Steve has continued to wear his Livestrong bracelet. We would often refer to it as his visual motivator and a sign that he could overcome anything. We made a pact to only take it off when Steve felt he had recovered enough that he was feeling like himself again. However, even once back to his regular life roles, Steve continued to wear the bracelet.

Thus, a dilemma arises after Armstrong's downfall. The Livestrong bracelet: to wear or not to wear? Steve is disappointed in Armstrong, frustrated that the cycling world has been misled and angry that the athlete he once idolized has been proven to be a fraud.

Steve removes the yellow wristband, refusing to wear or support Livestrong ever again. I am taken aback by his strong reaction. When I ask him about his decision, he tells me that honesty and integrity are imperative and that to be a hero, one must genuinely earn it.

Moving forward, we disregard one hero but are soon presented with another—one who has been through the most traumatic year of surgeries and ICU hospitalization imaginable. And although he doesn't see himself this way, Steve is also regarded as a hero by the VGH team. They ask us to attend their fundraising gala to demonstrate to their donors what a difference the ICU can make in achieving a positive outcome.

One year and four months to the day of his accident, we head to the Night of a Thousand Stars. Steve is working in Vancouver again, and I fly in the afternoon of the fundraiser. We dress up for the black-tie event, both of us looking healthy and elegant. We take a taxi to the Fairmont Hotel where the event is being held.

Steve and I stand in the cocktail lounge, people watching and feeling honoured to be a part of such an important event. We are guests at the ICU department table, sharing this beautiful evening with Dr. George I and the other doctors and nurses, most of whom we know. When we first arrive at our table, we are introduced to a young couple we've never met before. His name also happens to be Steve. Until he is called up, we don't realize that he is the motivational speaker of the evening and a true hero among heroes.

He limps slowly up to the stage and we listen in awe as his story unfolds. He was in his early twenties, working in the forestry industry felling trees when his accident occurred. Somehow, he became entangled in the heavy equipment and was dragged down the mountain. He spent most of his lengthy hospitalization in the ICU and endured more than seventy-two surgeries.

His story is overwhelming, even for a toughened hospital veteran like me. It's hard to hear of a young strong body battered beyond one's imagination. The younger Steve speaks with courage, charisma, and determination like I have never heard. We are completely humbled and inspired to be the finest versions of ourselves, to overcome and surpass huge obstacles, and to make the most of what life offers with humour, resolve, and gratitude.

The room is silent while he speaks, capped off with a triumphant applause. My Steve and I look at each other, hug, relieved to have overcome the worst. We are so fortunate to be in this amazing room, in a country with a wonderful health care system and dedicated health care providers. We went through a lot, but we are lucky indeed.

CHAPTER 23

Almost two years later May 2013 to July 2013. Heart surgery to heart broken

I T IS ALMOST two years since Steve's accident.

This May, we have a follow-up appointment to see Dr. Faud M, Steve's cardiac surgeon at Sunnybrook, to discuss the repair/replacement of his tricuspid heart valve and review the results of his recent esophageal echocardiogram and angiogram tests.

Dr. M is an extremely handsome, charismatic man who instils confidence in his patients. He joins us in the clinic room and asks if Steve's ears have been ringing, since he's been consistently bringing up Steve's case during rounds. He tells us that the team considers Steve a high-risk surgery due to his complex medical history.

Dr. M tells us that considering the severity of Steve's injuries, specifically the need for ECMO, he never should have recovered so well. He believes that Steve's premorbid healthy body and personality traits helped get him to this unlikely but amazing outcome. He confides that since he has come to know Steve, and to see how determined and motivated he is, he has been fighting to make my husband's case for surgery.

For the longest time, we have been functioning in survival mode. Steve seems to again believe that he is invincible and has been giving little thought to the past two years. We have just been trying to move forward with our lives. Most likely, not looking back or dwelling on our extremely traumatic experience has been a form of self-protection.

This appointment is a reality check for both of us, highlighting Steve's ongoing vulnerability, while reminding us of his miraculous outcome. It also stresses the possibility that the goals Steve has set for himself may not be realistic. Dr. M intimates that Steve's symptoms of tricuspid valve impairment are not typical. He and the rest of the team are concerned about the risks. As part of the workup to determine his candidacy for surgery, they need to assess his lung function due to his shortness of breath.

Steve is therefore referred for pulmonary function testing, as well as to a cardiology specialist who deals with unusual cases. Dr. M wants another opinion about whether Steve will be able to endure the surgery due to his multiple medical issues and to assess whether the benefits outweigh the risks. If Steve does not have the surgery, the left side of his heart will continue to enlarge and compensate for the right-side tricuspid regurgitation.

In other words, without surgery, Steve will present with increased cardiac issues and over time his shortness of breath will increase resulting in limited function and capacity and therefore reduced mobility. Steve is keen to go ahead with the surgery, despite the risks, so he can get on with his life and put this all behind him.

The year 2013, almost two years after Steve's accident, is a trying time in our relationship. Steve believes he is nearly back to his prior self; from my perspective, he remains quite different. Though he doesn't always let on, I think he remains frustrated because he's not as capable, strong, or athletic. His body has let him down.

He continues to be short of breath when active. He has back pain and when it's intense, he resorts to taking a Percocet to enable him to function. The right side of his body remains weaker, a mild hemiparesis, which is only visible to the discerning eye. He is also less tolerant of people, particularly the kids and me. I believe his cognitive filter is lacking and he now says what he thinks, regardless of whom he offends.

He is disappointed and frustrated—angry at himself, angry about what happened, angry that he is less capable, and angry that he no longer has the freedom to do what he would like. He is also angry with me. He has become impatient and is no longer willing to put in the hard work necessary for his physical recovery. Things have always come easy for Steve and this is no longer the case.

Although I know some of this must be evident to him, Steve won't admit this to himself or to me. He buries his emotions. He doesn't want to be reminded of the accident in any way, nor does he think about the impact it has had on us or discuss what he needs to do to get stronger and maintain his range of movement. He minimizes his limitations to anyone who asks. He says that he is perfect, and everything is fine.

He *wants* to believe this. He doesn't take ownership for his current situation or his future health. He no longer appears grateful for his life being saved and for the people around him, including me. He doesn't deal with any emotions arising from his medical situation, and he underestimates the impact of the accident and his miraculous recovery.

The kinder, softer, gracious man is buried deep down; on the surface, he is an impatient, selfish, and self-preserving individual, who is in complete denial. He has never worked through his anxieties and guilt about the accident (other than that one breakthrough night at VGH), nor his need to have risk, speed, and adrenaline in his life. He has lost his "freedom."

He can no longer run with the energy, breath support, and strength he had before the accident. He can't ride his motorcycle. He is stuck in a body that is not as compliant as before. I believe he is mad at himself for ruining his own life and feeling guilty for affecting all of ours. He understandably wants to move forward, to create a new future, and to forget the past. He deals with the free spirit inside him by distancing himself from all of us and running away from his own reality.

Steve is back to working and travelling at his "normal" workaholic pace. He has more responsibilities working for two companies. He starts spending more time away from home, working at the office based in Vancouver. This new environment feels liberating to him. No one there knows much about what happened to him, the old Steve, the Steve before the accident.

He doesn't share much with his colleagues. He can start fresh again. No one worries about his medical condition or knows his limitations. He is back to drinking vodka and Red Bull, while relying on energy drinks with significant amounts of caffeine to stay awake. To the non-discerning eye, Steve looks physically healthy and capable. He looks good for someone who has lung dysfunction, heart limitations, blood clotting issues, back pain, and weakness on one side of his body. He masks it well.

Still, he has recently experienced two emergency hospitalizations. The first was in Toronto, for a large blood clot in his leg, requiring him to go back on his blood thinners. The second time he was hospitalized in Vancouver due to his blood pressure plummeting to a critically low level. He passed out on the sidewalk while walking back to his hotel room and the paramedics were called.

The latter event was believed to be from severe dehydration after flying, followed by drinking vodka and Red Bull to stay awake for work. The doctor told me that Steve is lucky that he was in a public place at the time of the event, so that an ambulance was called. If he had been alone in his hotel room, he may not have survived this sudden severe drop in blood pressure. My resilience is waning because Steve minimizes each incident. I occasionally tell people not to be deceived by his facade, as the inner workings are not as stable as the outside appearance. My concern and constant worrying irritates him. Cognitively, he has made an incredible recovery, yet there are subtle changes in him that the kids and I notice. He has given up exercising with his trainer and with me. He wants to be free of being told what to do, of not being in control, of being reminded of his limitations.

I believe Steve needs professional support to move forward in a healthy way, and I suggest this to him. However, he thinks it's completely unnecessary. As far as he's concerned, he's recovered well and doesn't have any issues. He's not willing or interested in exploring what got him into this situation or the repercussions that followed. According to Steve, the accident and its effects are over.

It seems ironic to me that the city in which he became critically ill and developed PTSD is now the place where he feels the most comfortable. He buys himself a high-end mountain bicycle, which he keeps in Vancouver, and starts riding again. A small boutique hotel becomes his preferred home. He is well known in the hotel bar and restaurant, where the staff enjoy chatting with him and see him as a charming, successful, congenial man.

Despite his limitations, being in Vancouver and experiencing this new sense of freedom inspire his old sense of adventure. He is happy with this newfound life he has created, where he doesn't have to account to anyone, not family members or medical authorities. It is his free spirit resurfacing in a different way, and he feels on top of the world.

He is on a high following a very low period. He has become arrogant, cocky, uncaring, and separated from his current life at home. He believes he has earned the right to live his life as he pleases, with no regard for those who matter. It is likely a combination of phenomena which have caused Steve to change and become this person I really don't like.

Maybe this is his way of moving on and coping; maybe this is a form of denial; maybe he's running away from his reality; maybe we are reminders of the traumatic recent past; or maybe this is an exacerbation of his innate personality traits—i.e. his thrill-seeking behaviour, compounded on a mild brain injury.

I always believed that this life and death experience would make him grateful for everything he has. Unfortunately, the opposite has happened. He is turning away from all of us who have been there for him since the beginning. I am having a hard time dealing with this "new" Steve.

I did not sign up for this.

I try to deal with Steve's change as constructively as possible. I vacation with him in Vancouver. We ride bikes, take long walks on the seawall, eat out, and enjoy each other's company. Things are easier on vacation. So much has changed in our lives and I am not yet ready to confront him on his changed behaviour.

Family time and stability for my children are paramount to me, particularly after what we've been through, and I work hard to maintain this. We have a lot to deal with, including Steve's upcoming heart surgery. There will come a time to sort this all out, but now is not the right time. We are precariously riding through this cycle; it's easier to superficially manage, despite the bumps on the road.

Steve is not the only one suffering. About a year after his accident, I realize I need emotional support and an outlet, so I consult with a psychiatrist to help me come to terms with my emotions, fear, and anger over what happened. It is important for me to express how I am feeling to an unbiased person, without hurting someone I love. I need these sessions to work through my issues and to feel comfortable moving on and accepting our changed lives.

By July 2013, Linda, our close friend with leukemia, is now palliative. It is devastating to see her struggling with end-stage cancer. She deals with her illness with such insight, dignity, and care for her family. I feel this impacts Steve, making him confront his own mortality, fragility, and vulnerability—all the emotions he has compartmentalized and stored away.

Linda's illness is a wake-up call for Steve. He says: "I feel so guilty surviving my accident, my subsequent complications and it is Linda who is dying." He says that he feels he doesn't deserve to live and that Linda does. They are good friends and refer to each other as the "1% people," as they both seem to get the rare complications that only 1% of the population gets.

Steve is fortunate and pulls through. Linda is less fortunate and does not. Linda dies on July 22, 2013. We are all heartbroken.

CHAPTER 24

December 2013 to April 2014 surgery, life, death

I N THE LATE SUMMER, a cardiology specialist at Sunnybrook assesses Steve. He recommends going ahead with surgery. In his opinion, Steve will likely withstand the procedure, despite his known risks. The benefits of the surgery will improve his quality of life, preventing cardiac deterioration and enabling his heart to function somewhat normally. The medical team remains unsure whether Steve's shortness of breath is due to his lung or heart dysfunction.

We meet again with Steve's cardiac surgeon Dr. Faud M, and the plans are made for the upcoming operation. Steve requires a tricuspid valve replacement or repair, which involves open-heart surgery. This means that his chest will be opened and his heart stopped for a period of time, so that the surgeon can repair or replace the valve.

The damage to his valve can only be assessed during surgery and then the procedure required to deal with its functionality will be determined. Although this valve surgery is standard for a cardiac surgeon, Steve's high-risk case is not. The surgeons remain unsure about whether Steve will tolerate the procedure. The surgery will require the presence of two cardiac surgeons, Dr. Faud M and one of his colleagues, so that they can respond appropriately should any complications arise.

Once the surgery date is set, Steve enrols in a cardiac exercise programme at TRI (Toronto Rehab Institute), attending weekly classes for six months to prepare for surgery. I am relieved that he agrees to participate, as it will get him into the best possible condition before the procedure. This is a comprehensive programme, encompassing nutrition, as well as cardiac and strength training exercises. Steve will have to listen to the programme staff. It is a challenge and motivator for him; though he meets with a group, he trains at his own level.

Since the surgery isn't considered urgent, we delay it until February 2014, so the four of us can have a family vacation during the December holiday break. I want this to be a special time together, to relax, have fun and not focus on our next challenge. Symbolically, this vacation is important for me since we are once again facing the unknown and I'm not feeling as positive or optimistic as I should. Scarred from the past few years, I worry that Steve will have a difficult and lengthy recovery or, worse, that he won't survive.

We return from our week away and get back into our routines. I do my research regarding Steve's upcoming surgery. I like to be fully informed for what lies ahead. I research and over-analyse everything, which I admit may be a personality flaw. I know Steve has a tough and long recovery ahead and I want us to be prepared.

It seems the wake-up call from Linda's death is short-lived. One would imagine Steve would be more patient, understanding and grateful after what he's been through. Instead, he continues to struggle with his emotions and frustrations, stemming from his limited functioning.

He minimizes his upcoming surgery. He doesn't read up on the procedure or examine what it entails. He is again in denial and believes that he will be able to work from home within a week of his surgery, back to the Toronto office soon after that, and back to his happy place in Vancouver a few weeks later.

Steve plans his next few weeks accordingly, believing that this surgery is a small pothole to ride over from which he'll quickly recover. He believes his life will continue with little interruption. The fact that he doesn't dwell on his upcoming surgery may be a positive trait, at least for him, but I don't think he is being realistic by refusing to confront his medical issues. In fact, he is quite angry with me for reminding him about the seriousness of the operation, the long recovery, and future limitations.

When I challenge him on his attitude and lack of preparation, he accuses me of being overly protective and unnecessarily anxious.

He responds by saying; "Dans, I'm fine. It's not a big deal. Stop making a fuss. In fact, I don't think we even need to tell anyone about my heart surgery. I will recover quickly, be back working in a week and travelling again soon."

It is so frustrating for me. He is feeling invincible again, denying reality and telling me my concern is all in my head. I know that his facade that "he is fine' does not fully represent how his body is really functioning. He can fool himself and others into believing that he is "perfect," his term to describe himself. I am not that gullible or naive.

When we arrive for Steve's pre-surgery workup appointment, the anaesthesiologist enters the waiting room with Steve's chart in hand. She looks around for her patient and then leaves. When she returns, finally realizing who we are, she is in complete disbelief. She tells us that Steve's appearance doesn't match what is written in his chart. She can't believe someone with Steve's medical history could present so "healthy."

Steve's open-heart surgery goes ahead as planned on February 24, 2014. I no longer have the energy, commitment, and focus that I had during his initial hospitalization. I am burned out. I feel grateful that this time Josh and Gabi are with me and can shoulder some of the responsibility of worrying about and taking care of Steve. My usual source of support, my parents, have both developed their own medical issues, and it's hard for them to be as involved.

Josh, Gabi, Maxine, and I sit together in the cardiac surgery waiting area, anxiously trying to pass the time. His surgery is smoother and shorter than expected and he comes through this surgery in his premorbid style, always ahead of the game. His tricuspid valve is repaired, which carries a much better long-term outcome than if he required a replacement.

He is now ventilated and in the cardiac ICU. He makes good progress and within two days is weaned off the ventilator and moved onto the cardiac floor. Despite some complications with his blood clotting, he does quite well and is discharged after eight days. He is sent home with a strict programme to increase his physical activity, which he must adhere to rigorously.

Even though the surgery is successful, Steve's recovery is slow and painful. This is quite a shock to him and nothing like he anticipated. He has intense chest pain as his wound heals, and he is frail and weak once again. He becomes depressed and quite emotional. He questions many things, including why he survived. He also feels guilty about his attitude and behaviour over the past year.

He is dependent on me again, and although this doesn't feel good for him, he seems grateful that I'm here. He sleeps a lot and isn't very motivated or capable of doing much. He can't drive for six weeks and so he is limited to the house and to travelling with me. He is disappointed in himself and despondent about his situation.

This is a huge setback for Steve, but we've come this far, and there's no use in dwelling on it. He starts doing a few tiny laps around our living room. Even this small distance wipes him out. Slowly, he begins to make progress, becoming less short of breath and gaining some strength. It is quite cold outside, so we go to a mall to increase his walking distance and endurance.

We are a team again (albeit a burned-out one). My family works to help Steve rebuild his strength. It takes six weeks for Steve to feel relief from most of his pain and to get somewhat stronger. He re-enrols in the cardiac rehabilitation programme at TRI. This time, his pace and progress are slower but steady. It takes another six months for him to return to his activities of daily living and at least a year to fully recover from this surgery.

I think with this tricuspid repair Steve got his heart back, functionally and emotionally, literally, and figuratively. We see glimpses of the old Steve—the Steve who cares, whom we like and respect, the Steve who wants to be home with his family. He no longer feels invincible; in fact, he feels quite fragile. He is willing to go for some professional help to deal with his fears, his attitude, and to try to understand his previously risky lifestyle.

He is not as interested in travelling as much, working as excessively or being the free spirit that he once was. This Steve wants to move forward to a much healthier, more acceptable, and peaceful place. He is no longer compelled to find his next adrenaline rush, intense reckless experience, or extreme sensation or challenge. He works through his guilt and misdirected anger and comes out on the other side being his best person yet.

He is once again grateful, wanting to improve on his approach to life and focus on his family. He now considers us to be the safe, comfortable, and nurturing people that he needs. We are a solid family again, burnt around the edges, but doing quite well.

Josh is now working full time in an amazing job in media, and he is in a solid relationship with his boyfriend Adam. They live together in downtown Toronto. Gabi and her boyfriend Jamie are back at university working hard. My children can get on with their lives and finally put this trauma behind them.

There are still a few potholes in the road that continue to derail us, some more devastating than others. Four weeks after Steve's open-heart surgery, my dad becomes critically ill with melanoma metastases in his stomach and liver. He is in Sunnybrook Hospital for six gruesome weeks.

During these six overwhelming and traumatic weeks, Steve takes on the responsibility of being and sitting with my dad, even though my husband is still in the early stages of his own recovery. My dad has always been there for Steve and now he can support him in return.

Two surgeries later and following so many complications, my incredibly special dad dies in my arms, with my mother, brother Paul, Steve, and Josh beside him. Gabi is in the middle of her final exams, away at school. Gabi and Jamie had been with him a few days earlier to say their heartbreaking goodbyes. His death is brutal for all of us. We lose this incredibly vibrant, brilliant, and exceptional man from our lives.

Steve and my father bond during this period, with one of them healing slowly and the other dying rapidly. We deal with this loss together as a family, sad to have lost my father, but happy to have Steve back. He is concerned, involved and empathic, and working on improving his physical, mental, and emotional well-being. Steve comes through completely for my dad, for himself, and for all of us.

CHAPTER 25

July 16, 2015 Four years later

STEVE AND I are in the car on our way to a doctor's appointment. I casually mention that it's exactly four years to the day of his accident. I want to mark the date and acknowledge how far we have come but I anticipate that Steve will dismiss this comment, as always. He still doesn't want to talk about the accident, the emotional and physical toll it has taken, or anything to do with that time in his life. He wants to move forward and forget.

I am totally surprised—stunned actually—when he replies, "It's time to go see Frank." The truck driver who found him lying on that rural road in Yukon. "We'll be in Vancouver. Let's just drop in to see Frank and Sandy. It's time to go meet them and thank Frank for finding and saving me on the road."

And that's all it takes. Full circle and four years later, we are going to "drop in" to see Frank and Sandy in rural Yukon, approximately 2,500 kilometres from where we will be in Vancouver. In true Steve style, within days he has emailed Sandy about the dates and planned our route. Steve seems almost as excited as when he was planning his motorcycle rides.

This time we will rent an SUV to travel the long distances on the Alaska Highway and the rural, gravel roads. It is a long way north and Steve planned the journey, distances, timing, places to stay, and scenic routes. I can feel his excitement, something I haven't felt in a while.

On Friday, July 31, we fly to Vancouver. We relax over the long weekend and Steve works for two days. We are both excited and perhaps a bit apprehensive to start our adventure. He has always wanted me to join him on a road trip, but I never wanted to go on his motorcycle. Now we are finally doing it together, safely, on four wheels.

On August 5, I send my very last message to the original group I shared information with four years ago. I tell them of our travel plans and what we hope to see. I have added some people to the group but sadly cannot message Linda or my father.

On Friday night, we fly into Fort St. John, a small town in Northern British Columbia and pick up a solid SUV and leave early the next morning on our road trip. Steve's itinerary is precise and well planned, with long days and extensive distances. I have left everything for him to arrange. I am just along for the ride.

We travel over two thousand kilometres by car, through two provinces and two countries, in just three days. Through Alaska and the Rockies, we see magnificent mountain ranges, forests and lakes on and off the Alaska Highway. We see some wildlife, including brown bears. Knowing that this is bear territory, I imagine how frightening it must have been for Steve. I marvel again at the wonder of Steve's SPOT for saving his life.

We planned to arrive at Johnson's Crossing, Yukon, late Friday afternoon August 7. Sandy and Frank bought a small lodge here two years earlier, leaving their home in Faro. Johnson's Crossing has a population of forty, and we are going to stay the night at their lodge. We are both excited and apprehensive.

In the past, I emailed with Sandy in the early months following Steve's accident and briefly about a year ago when she told us about their move. When I ask Steve about Frank, he can't remember much. I am curious about who these people are and what Frank looks like. I have always wondered how he managed to lift Steve into the truck. Will we get on together? Will it be awkward, emotional, surreal? Will we have much to say or share? I am unsure how Steve will react, as he still doesn't show much emotion.

On our way from Muncho Lake, we take time out from the drive for a short swim in the Laird River Hot Springs. There is still quite a distance to go. At Watson Lake, we do a detour to see the beginning of the symbolic "Campbell Highway," the gravel road where Steve crashed. We plan to drive on just a small stretch of the road, about ten kilometres as it feels like a bit of bad karma to drive on this road.

We are both apprehensive when we turn onto the road until we realize this part of the road has been recently paved. Steve is disappointed. He wants to show me what the gravel road and thick bush really looked like when he had his accident. So we keep driving onwards, hoping to find the gravel road while re-evaluating whether we should continue or turn around and go back to the Alaska Highway.

About forty kilometres in, we come across a construction crew, then ungraded sand and then finally the old gravel road. We look at each other, fully on the same page; we know what we must do. We have come so far, we might as well drive the entire stretch of the road that Steve rode on until we reach Ross River, and only then will we turn around and drive to Johnson's Crossing.

This is our one and only opportunity to see this section of road. We will likely never be in this area again. So, although we have not planned it, in this moment it feels like the right choice. We are meant to drive this road and we are meant to do this now. We will travel almost an extra six hundred kilometres on rugged, treacherous sand and gravel roads so that we can share this experience. It will take us another nine and a half hours of driving, with a short stop in Ross River to refuel and see the nursing station, before we can reach Frank and Sandy later tonight.

The road all looks the same and we feel that finding the exact spot of Steve's accident will be impossible. In my computer bag are some notes, as well as the RCMP report that I just located the week before. It occurs to me that the police report contains the coordinates of the accident.

Now we have the exact location on the road where Steve crashed, exactly where he lay for that hour and a half before Frank found him. Steve puts the longitude and latitude coordinates into the GPS. I can't even begin to explain the mix of emotions we both experience. It is exciting, nerve-wracking, and strange. After all, it is just road and bush, all looking the same, and yet it is incredibly symbolic for us. It is a traumatic spot on the road, which has changed our lives forever.

It's been raining today, just like the day of Steve's accident. As we approach the location on the road, with ten kilometres to go, our apprehension intensifies. We count down the kilometres until we finally get to zero. We have reached our "destination," the barren spot on the road.

The rain has stopped. It is just a gravel road, with rocks, trees, and thick bush, the same sights we have seen the whole way. We climb out of the car and look around; we hug and hold each other. I am quite emotional, with tears in my eyes. Steve's face is taut. I say, "We made it, Steve . . . we found it . . . you made it, you survived, despite the odds! You are invincible!"

We laugh, an outpouring of relief, tears running down my face. I swear that there might even be a glisten of a tear in Steve's eyes. We share this extraordinary place and moment together. I take pictures of the road and of Steve with a big smile on his face and his arms up in the air.

I collect some small rocks from the side of the road and build a mound on the shoulder of the road, marking Steve's accident site. By chance, I find a rock which has two white circular lines naturally marked onto it. The rock looks like a target. I place it on top of my pile of rocks. It is symbolic for me, for us, and it represents Steve's place on the road.

This is where he survived. This time we are here together and this time the experience is positive. We get back into our car and continue our journey with a sense of relief and accomplishment. The tension and apprehension dissipate. This has been a trip four years in the making.

The landscape is even more spectacular here with lush forests, clear rivers and lakes, valleys, snow-capped mountains, and wildlife sightings (including a few more brown bears). There is not a car, person, or structure in sight.

It is truly breathtaking here, and we take in the beauty together. I now understand Steve's passion for riding in such beautiful and unspoiled terrain. What's not to love? We reach Ross River at six with an empty gas tank. If we are too late to get gas, we will have to spend the night in the car. The sign says they close at five, but fortunately they are kind enough to open the only gas tank so we can fill up.

Ross River has a population of 313. The Kaska First Nation community live in this area and hunt, fish, and act as adventure guides. This was the first medical triage stop on Steve's journey, where the ambulance of volunteer paramedics took him and where he was first seen by a nurse.

We go to the Health Centre. The main doors are unfortunately closed since it is already Friday evening. I have since learned that being a rural unit, primary health care nurses here provide daily clinics for medical treatment, community health programmes, and twenty-four-hour emergency services (likely via a pager system or after-hours emergency number). They respond to highway accidents by sending an ambulance with volunteer paramedics, just as in Steve's case. It is meaningful for us to see this unit, as it is another stop on Steve's journey.

It takes us another three and a half hours to reach Johnson's Crossing, driving along the treacherous dirt South Canol Road. Amazingly, we see a grizzly bear standing upright on the road. It is the most daunting sight. I would not have liked to have been alone on the side of the road as Steve had been, in the presence of such a large predatory animal. I am a city girl; the thought of bears roaming the area is completely foreign and frightening to me.

We are now close to the home of Frank and Sandy. They are sitting outside in front of the lodge, talking to another couple, as we drive up. Frank stands up. He is a tall and solid man, rugged, with a ruddy red face, big smile, and a large bushy moustache. While he looks like a Viking trucker to me, he's also the warmest and most humble man. Sandy is petite, vivacious, easy-going. There is not one awkward moment between us, all total strangers; there is only warmth, friendship, graciousness, and conversation.

Steve and Frank shake hands and then hug. Both men have tears brimming in their eyes. Initially, they underplay the significance, both stating that the whole thing is not a big deal. Yet I can sense the emotion and meaning of this moment, how grateful each man is for the other. Sandy welcomes us, hugs us hello, and tells us how happy they are that we have come all this way, after all this time, to see them. She says she believes these men were meant to meet.

They serve us a delicious homemade BBQ dinner and we sit chatting until one am. We come from two different worlds and yet we have so much to talk about. Over the course of the evening, Sandy looks at Frank as if asking his permission and tells us they want to share a story with us. They both have tears running down their cheeks as Sandy recounts, with Frank's input, what happened to Frank two years before Steve's accident.

I will do my best to repeat the story as closely as I can. Sandy and Frank were married six years ago. Theirs is an amazing love story: a chance meeting at nineteen, a hard working life, different relationships, different cities and finally marriage over twenty years later. Their love and respect for each other is incredibly strong. Sandy is extremely protective over her large, rugged trucker husband.

She tells the story of Frank driving home from one of his long trucking jobs in the freezing, icy winter, when he encountered a bad stretch of road. I can feel their sadness as Sandy speaks. As Frank was driving, he spotted a pickup truck heading towards him. The small truck skids on the icy road, straightening out momentarily and then sliding on the ice again, smashing into Frank's large rig.

The driver was a young twenty-four-year-old man, a "kid" as they call him, a technician working on an oil rig. He died on that road in Frank's arms. Sandy tells us that Frank was so traumatized by this young man's death that he found it hard to return to trucking. She says the accident changed him. He was deeply disturbed by what happened and felt somewhat responsible that he couldn't save "the kid." The police report stated that road conditions and the young driver's speed likely caused the accident. This didn't help Frank cope with the tragedy, which continued to plague him.

Two years later, Frank had returned to trucking and was on his way home on the Campbell Highway. It was a rainy day in summer. If you recall from earlier in the story, Frank was not meant to be on the road at that time of the day. It was by sheer chance that he was driving his truck during dusk on his way home to dinner with Sandy.

It was by utter fortune for Steve that Frank had been delayed in Watson Lake and came upon Steve. There, lying just ahead on the side of the road, was a person who appeared unable to move, due to what looked like an accident. Frank was stunned and felt he couldn't go through another experience like he had two years before.

Now we understand why it was so important for Frank and Sandy to stay in touch after Steve's accident. They needed to know that Steve was okay, to help Frank cope and move forward. Two accidents, the first fatal and the second nearly fatal, were too much for Frank to deal with.

Sandy's initial email to us on July 18, 2011, which I included earlier in this story, now seems so much more meaningful:

> *I am Frank's wife Sandy and we are both so thankful your husband is going to be fine and is now in surgery. Words cannot describe the relief Frank feels now that he has spoken with you and knows that Steven is going to be fine. I called the RCMP yesterday because Frank was beside himself with worry, he is a very kind and gentle soul my husband and this has shaken him up a little.*

Sandy's words resonate with me now. Steve and I sit quietly processing what they have shared with us. We are all shaken by Frank's experience and the chance of it all. Sandy turns to both Steve and me and says, "You see, although Frank saved Stephen, Stephen enabled Frank to heal. Stephen saved Frank too!"

She tells us that just after Steve's accident, she told Frank that things were going to be okay now. He couldn't save the first young man, but he was able to save this one. She said she believes that these two men were meant to cross paths and would forever be bonded by their experience.

We leave early the next morning to finish our round trip to Alaska, Steve's special place, the pot of gold at the end of the rainbow. Frank is working early on the road, helping a friend. At six am in the morning, Frank knocks on our door. He has come to hug us goodbye. It has been an incredibly special meeting, cathartic for all of us. Two men, from very different walks of life, brought together by time and location, hug goodbye. We are forever grateful to Frank.

With these thoughts in mind, Steve and I set off on our long trip home. Our shared journey has brought us closer together. As we pass through the untouched wilderness, we see both the beauty and danger in the remote land. With all that we've endured, we are better prepared to tackle life's challenges, we are at peace, and we are excited for the opportunities that lay ahead.

Epilogue

I T HAS NOW been a decade since the most difficult time of our lives. Somehow, through all the challenges we have endured, I realize how fortunate we are. How many besides Steve can say they overcame a "zero percent chance" of survival?

We are particularly lucky for the miracles that led to saving Steve. Sometimes I wonder what would have happened if the SPOT device hadn't landed within arm's reach or if the loose bony fragments hadn't missed Steve's spinal column or if Frank's plans hadn't changed leading him to Steve's side. There's no use in dwelling on what could have happened. If Steve's ordeal has taught us anything it's to live in the moment. We don't know what the future will bring. We can only face life's obstacles as they come.

Unfortunately, there are some challenges that can't be overcome. As mentioned earlier, late in Steve's recovery, we lost both our friend Linda and my father. Steve's ongoing health concerns made it difficult for me to properly mourn these major losses in my life.

Our next loss was not a person but rather a place. Due to Steve's limitations, our family cottage was no longer as appealing. Steve could no longer ski or drive the boat, due to the impact of the waves/wakes on his spine, and he struggled to perform the maintenance necessary for upkeep. With Josh and Gabi moving forward with their lives, we made the difficult decision to sell our piece of heaven, my escape.

Maddy, our beautiful golden retriever, loved the cottage nearly as much as she loved her family. After a wonderful long life, she developed a nasal tumour causing her to choke on her own blood. Thinking of her quality of life, we made the difficult decision to put her to sleep. Steve and I had always said that if the quality of Maddy's life was ever compromised, we would help end her life peacefully and with dignity. As a family, we made this decision together quickly and easily, unlike my experience with Steve.

Just when we felt like we couldn't endure any more, in May 2019, my independent, incredible, feisty mom experienced congestive heart failure and died suddenly at home. How lucky was she that she never knew she died? It was terribly shocking and sad for all of us. She was literally my favourite person in the world, my backbone, support system, and confidant. She was my children's "other mother," so youthful and full of life.

When she died, her dog remained by her side, protecting her, as the paramedics, police, coroner, and funeral home staff attended to her body. Like myself, he could not imagine life without her.

With my parents gone, things will never be the same. I am sad neither of them got to read this book, but perhaps it's for the better. They wouldn't want to relive the events. It would have just made them sad, frustrated, and anxious. They believed in moving forward.

Despite all our losses, our family continues to grow. Josh works successfully in media. He and his partner Kyle live in their home in Toronto, with their menagerie of pets, mainly rescues. Gabi graduated from university and became an occupational therapist, inspired in part by the functional component to Steve's recovery. Jamie and Gabi are getting married and live with their golden retriever puppy Wally.

In addition to adding Kyle and Jamie to our family, we now have two delicious goldendoodle fur babies, twin sisters Hallie and Millie. "Our girls" bring immense joy, humour, and love into our lives.

I continue to work as a Pilates/movement instructor, building my studio and developing my skills. I am grateful that many of my clients who supported me during Steve's accident still attend my classes so regularly.

Finally, no update would be complete without describing Steve's incredible progress. He is grateful to be alive, though it's difficult for him to express. He can't look back. It's too painful and leaves him feeling vulnerable. He moves forward the way he knows how, by working hard and playing hard.

Steve's office chair is his new motorcycle, and he rides it frequently. I believe no one works as hard as he does. He joined Deciem, a young

Canadian skin care company that shook up the cosmetics industry with drama so intense it makes Steve's journey seem uncomplicated.

Steve was hired as the CFO and later transitioned into the position of COO of this thriving "abnormal" beauty company with over 1,400 employees worldwide. I know he is no "ordinary" senior executive, as his rise has been nothing short of miracles. The steel rod in his spine, his compromised lung, and his scars are the faint reminders of his history. He now acts with purpose, focus, resourcefulness, strategy, and exceptional execution. He communicates eloquently and writes brilliantly. He delegates and problem solves. He is most loved and respected.

His abilities, in contrast to just nine years ago, are incredible. I recall when he couldn't organize his thoughts, turn himself in bed, walk or feed himself. He was paranoid and suffering from PTSD. At the time, we were just hoping he'd survive. Never did I dream he'd rise so high again.

Leisure is now Steve's work. However, to keep active, we go on long walks with our four-legged girls. He rides his indoor and outdoor bicycles when he has time and works out in my studio when motivated. He is now fully aware of the huge risks that come with motorcycle riding and would never dare sit on that saddle again.

It's taken Steve many years to recover from the depth of his injuries, which he's done faster and with more tenacity than most. Despite a broken spine, with significant metal hardware, mild shortness of breath on exertion, his scars and subtle neurological impairments, Steve is back to being the "Bionic Man," our real-life superhero. His heart is now in the right place. He is grateful and appreciative of his experience and everyone who supported him.

If you saw him now, you'd never know of his past. He is strong and handsome. He has more salt than pepper in his full head of hair (only I lost my hair). He is funny and articulate. He has sheer grit, determination, and at least nine lives. He is a fighter.

Steve's trauma has undoubtedly left a lasting imprint on our relationship. In some ways we have grown closer. We were a team for so long, committed and trusting as we crossed the finish line together. This shared experience has bonded us forever.

In other ways, the impact and stress of the accident and his recovery have been destructive for me. I have developed a fear of loss and anticipate the possibility of further loss. I am always waiting for the "other shoe to drop," the inevitable, undesirable event to occur. I have lived on automatic pilot for so long. I now work with an incredibly supportive psychiatrist, with the focus being cognitive behavioural therapy. She has helped me understand Steve's actions and behaviours, redefine myself, and advocate for myself. She has shown me how to be in the present and mindful, to "ride the wave" and not waste energy on possibilities.

I am a work in progress, rebuilding my life with the beliefs that I am resourceful and resilient. I am able to both support Steve's goals and pursue my own. My life is now healthy, active, and peaceful.

I made the best decisions I could while facing the hardest challenges of my life. Were my decisions always correct? Maybe, maybe not. Even these many years later, it remains hard for me to say. I'm sure everyone will have their own opinion. My children, particularly Gabi, are not ready to open these old wounds. Like their father, they have compartmentalized this part of their lives and shut the door. I think back to my wise mom's advice: "Danielle, you can only do the best *you* can do and that is good enough."

We realize we are fortunate for what we have. There were so many points in Steve's journey where we were just hopeful he would survive. We are incredibly lucky that he pulled through and overwhelmingly astounded at his recovery. It took immense work to get to where he is today and Steve and I remain incredibly grateful to everyone who helped and supported us along the way.

Today, many years since the accident, I sit in my backyard and finish writing the end of this story. Steve has just come back from a forty-kilometre ride on his bicycle. He is proud, strong, handsome, and fit. Who would have thought that after years of trying to cycle back from trauma and crisis, Steve would be back on a two wheeler with a healthy body and mind and the wind in his face?

A note to the reader

'VE DONE MY best to relay the story accurately. All descriptions, quotes, and events are described as I remember them. It is understood that human memory is not perfect. To minimize errors, I've used primary sources (phone calls, emails, text messages, group chats, medical records, etc.) whenever possible.

While coping with Steve's tragedy, I was constantly updating friends and family. These messages have proven invaluable when writing the book. I have also done countless hours of research, used my own experience as a speech-language pathologist, and spoken with friends and family who were with me during the journey. Combining these various sources has led to a more accurate and detailed account.

When written correspondences are included, I've italicized them to set them out from the text. Some quotes have been slightly abridged for brevity or edited for grammar; however, most written correspondences are presented in full.

To help maintain privacy, I have referred to Steve's team of therapists by their first names. With regard to his medical team, I've referred to them by their first name and the first letter of their last name (e.g. Dr. George I). When the same physician is mentioned multiple times in a row, in subsequent mentions I only use the initial (e.g. Dr. I).

Glossary of selected medical terms

Acute hypoxemic respiratory failure: Critical illness resulting from the lack of sufficient oxygen levels in the blood. It is uncommon and often fatal.

Alteplase infusion: Is an enzyme to break up and dissolve blood clots that can block arteries. It is used in the treatment of acute heart attack or pulmonary embolism.

Anticoagulation therapy: The usage of medication to prevent blood clots.

Aspiration pneumonia: A condition that results when one inhales food, stomach acid, or saliva into the lungs.

Bed flow/patient flow: The monitoring of the movement of a patient within a health care facility or between facilities.

BiPAP (Bi-level positive airway pressure): A machine to help push air into the lungs if you have trouble breathing. It is positive pressure ventilation, as the device helps open lungs with this air pressure.

Blood urea nitrogen levels (BUN): Urea nitrogen is a normal waste product that the body creates after eating. The liver breaks down the proteins in food and creates BUN. The liver releases substances into the blood and eventually lands up in the kidneys. When kidneys are not functioning, they have trouble removing BUN. If levels are off the normal range, it could mean the kidneys or liver is not working properly.

Bradycardia: A heart rate that is too slow.

Burst T6 fracture: An injury to the thoracic spine in which the vertebral body is severely compressed.

Camp Manitou: It is a children's sleep-over camp for boys and girls, located in the Muskoka—Parry Sound region, Ontario, Canada. It brings together a diverse community of campers and staff from around the world.

Cannula: A thin tube inserted into a vein or body cavity.

Cardiogenic shock: This cardiac shock happens when the heart cannot pump enough blood and oxygen to the brain and other vital organs.

CT scans (computed tomography scan): A diagnostic tool that uses a series of X-ray images taken from across the body to create a cross-sectional look of the bones, blood vessels, and soft tissues.

Central line: A type of catheter that allows multiple IV fluids to be given and blood to be drawn.

DVT (deep vein thrombosis): A condition that occurs when a blood clot forms in a deep vein in the body, usually in the legs.

Delirium: A change in the brain that leads to mental confusion and a disruption of emotional functioning.

Dialysis: A treatment that cleans the blood and removes excess fluid from the body when the kidneys are no longer able to function.

ECMO (extracorporeal membrane oxygenation): Known as extracorpeal life support, a technique/life-support machine providing prolonged cardiac and respiratory support to people whose heart and lungs are unable to function in order to sustain life.

EMS: Emergency medical services, a system providing emergency medical care.

Endotracheal tube: Is a flexible tube placed through the nose or mouth into the trachea (windpipe) to help a patient breathe.

Heparin infusion: The delivery of an anticoagulant medication through a vein.

Hoyer lift: A electrical or hydraulic sling lift device that helps transfer people between a bed and a chair.

Hypoxic event: The lack of sufficient oxygen to the brain.

ICU (intensive care unit): A unit of the hospital which treats critically ill patients. It is staffed with specifically trained health care professionals and contains sophisticated monitoring equipment.

ICUAW (intensive care unit-acquired weakness): Extreme weakness brought about by time in a critical care setting.

ICU psychosis/delirium: A brain disorder in which patients in a critical care setting may experience. It often shows up suddenly with features such as trouble focusing, sudden changes in behaviour and confusion. For most people delirium doesn't last long.

Interventional radiology: A specialty that provides image-guided diagnosis and treatment of disease.

Intra-arterial tPA: An emergency treatment following an ischemic stroke that can reduce the severity and improve the outcome of the stroke.

IVC filter: A small device placed in the inferior vena cava (a large vein) to prevent blood clots from going up into the lungs.

Multiple organ systems failure: When the inflammation from a severe infection or injury causes dysfunction in two or more organ systems. This can be fatal.

Occupational therapist (OT): A health care professional who provides the skills to enable an individual to engage in activities and tasks of daily living. They focus on the assessment and treatment of physical, cognitive, perceptual, and psychosocial function.

OHIP (Ontario Health Insurance Plan): The government run health care insurance programme for Ontarians.

OR: The operating room in a hospital, where surgeries are performed.

Ototoxicity: Drug or chemical damage to the inner ear which can lead to hearing and/or balance problems.

Patient controlled analgesia (PCA): Is a pain management method that allows the patient to control the amount of pain medicine used, by pressing a button on a computerized pump.

Physiotherapist (PT): A health care professional who assesses and treats patients to maintain, improve, or restore physical functioning and mobility, alleviate pain, and prevent physical dysfunction.

Pneumothorax: This is a collapsed lung when air leaks into the space between the space between your lung and chest wall.

Proprioception: It is the sense of self movement and body position. It's the body's ability to sense movement, action, and location. It's present in every muscle movement.

PTSD (post-traumatic stress disorder): A mental health condition triggered by a terrifying event and leading to symptoms of flashbacks, nightmares, and anxiety.

Pulmonary embolism: The blockage of a major blood vessel in the lung, usually from a blood clot.

Quadriplegia: A type of spinal cord injury involving all four limbs and the torso.

RCMP (Royal Canadian Mounted Police): The federal and national police force in Canada.

Respiratory therapist (RT): A health care professional who works therapeutically with people who have acute critical conditions, cardiac and pulmonary disease. They treat problems with breathing and airway function.

Ross River Health Centre: This is a primary care walk-in/outpatient clinic in the province of Yukon. Services include dispensing specific medications and twenty-four-hour emergency services, as well as responding to highway accidents with ambulance.

Serum creatinine level: The amount of creatinine, which is a breakdown product of creatine phosphate from muscle and protein metabolism, should be stable in the blood. An increased level may mean poor kidney function.

Speech-language pathologist (SLP): A health care professional working in the evaluation, diagnosis, and treatment of communication and cognitive disorders, voice and swallowing disorders.

SPOT: A GPS safety device delivering reliable satellite location-based tracking, messaging, and lifesaving SOS technology.

Spinal step-down unit: A unit in the hospital that treats patients with spinal cord injuries and provides an intermediate level of care between the ICU and a general medical/surgical ward.

St. John's Rehab: A portion of Sunnybrook Health Sciences Centre devoted to rehabilitation.

Substitute decision-maker: The person(s) who is entitled by law to make health decisions on behalf of an incapable person.

Sunnybrook: The hospital (Sunnybrook Health Sciences Centre) where Steve received treatment once back in Toronto.

Tachypneic: A condition that refers to rapid breathing.

T5: T5 Spinous process fracture is a break or crack in the back part of the (T5) thoracic vertebra.

T6: Burst T6 vertebra is injury to the thoracic spine in which the vertebral body (of T6) is severely compressed. They typically occur from a motor vehicle accident or fall from a height.

Tissue plasminogen activator (tPA): It is a protein involved in the breakdown of clots.

Transaminases level: A body marker that helps detect the presence of injury to the liver.

Tricuspid heart valve: This valve is on the right side of the heart, separating the upper and lower chambers, and allows deoxygenated blood to flow through both of the chambers.

Tricuspid valve repair or replacement: There are several surgical techniques to repair the damaged tricuspid valve in the heart. Replacement takes out the badly damaged tricuspid valve and replaces it with a new valve. Tricuspid valve surgery traditionally involves open-heart surgery (opening of the chest bone).

VGH (Vancouver General Hospital): The hospital where Steve received much of his acute treatment.

VAC (vacuum-assisted closure) pump: A method that uses the controlled negative pressure of a vacuum to promote healing of certain types of wounds.

Whitehorse General Hospital: Is a largest hospital in Yukon, in the city of Whitehorse, providing emergency and in/out patient care.

Vital signs: The four main signs routinely monitored are body temperature, pulse rate, respiration rate (rate of breathing), and blood pressure.

Acknowledgements

THE OUTCOME OF our story may have been quite different if it weren't for our health care system and all these incredible professionals who work within it. Their work to restore physical and mental health is extremely meaningful and life changing.

The Canadian Universal Health Care system: We are beyond thankful for living in Canada and being privileged to have benefitted from the unwavering, dependable, and accessible health care that was afforded to Stephen every step of the way. Forever grateful.

To all the doctors and nurses whose expertise, caring, and belief in Stephen's life and recovery, I can't thank you enough. Particularly the brilliant and compassionate Dr. George Isac, Medical Director of Vancouver General Hospital (VGH) ICU, to whom we are always thankful for you being there for us in the right place at the right time. Dr. Robert Lee, Orthopaedic and Spinal Surgeon, Wellington Hospital, London, for being so skilled, involved, and supportive throughout. Dr. Morad Hameed, Critical Care VGH, whose kindness and considerate manner raised our spirits. Dr. Paul Marik (my brother), one of a kind pulmonary and critical care specialists, whose only goal in life is quality medical care and to save patients at any cost. Dr. Homer Tien, Trauma Surgeon Sunnybrook Health Sciences Centre, whose efforts enabled a smooth transfer to Sunnybrook and whose pragmatic approach instilled confidence in me when taking over Steve's care. And then Dr. Faud Moussa, Cardiac Surgery, Sunnybrook Health Sciences Centre, whose dedication to his patients, charisma, and determination to fight for Steve's surgery have left an everlasting impression.

I am most grateful for all the allied health care workers, the physiotherapists, occupational therapists, speech pathologists, respiratory therapists, and social workers who played a part in Steve's recovery. Illana, friend and social worker, who saw us through many dark moments and with skill and humour, facilitated our return home and continued to support us through our journey in Sunnybrook.

No words to describe how grateful we are to Frank, our guardian angel, and Sandy Ruether, his exceptional wife. The RCMP officers who went beyond "the call of duty."

This story wouldn't have become a book without the interest, encouragement, support, and effort of some incredible people. To those who steered me in the right direction and helped me turn my story into this book, I am so grateful.

Linda Lewis, previously editor of *Today's Parent* and *More Magazine Canada*. Linda encouraged my early thoughts about writing this story, planned to edit once written, and always had such an honest and comfortable relationship with Stephen. I cherished our friendship and will always remember her smile, determination, and the years of girlfriend fun we had. To all the beautiful sunflowers out there.

Booth Savage, Canadian film, stage, and television actor. My real friend who was willing to read over five hundred pages of the earliest draft, overflowing with dialogue and thoughts. He gave me the most beneficial advice, in his true direct style, by asking me whom I was writing this for—family and friends or anyone beyond this group. And so began the major editing.

Leora Eisen, Linda's identical twin sister, documentary director, and writer, known for *The Nature of Things*. Leora, my friend for life, without a second thought took over Linda's wish to edit the manuscript. She helped me deliver a more skilfully written story, with fresh eyes, thoughtful feedback, and introductions to literary agents.

Michael Levine, Canada's "superagent" and foremost entertainment lawyer, who gave me sound advice, provided me with book proposal guidelines, and took the time to read and give general feedback.

Jared Cappel, professional writer, underwriter, editor, with a special interest in medicolegal reports. His writing has appeared in many venues.

His invaluable detailed editing and writing of previous drafts of the manuscript have enabled the story to be prepared and polished, ready to catch the eye of a publisher.

re:books . . . Rebecca Eckler, my priceless publisher RE:BOOKS, Founder and Publisher of RE:BOOKS, Canadian writer of columns, blogs, a newsletter, and author of books. I am beyond grateful to you for giving me a shot, for believing in my story and knowing that this could be a book worthy of publication. You are an absolute cheerleader for me and all female authors, forming an incredible community of book writers and readers.

Deanna McFadden, my indispensable and most congruous editor. You are an incredible resource and writing coach. This amazing journey working together has been one of respect, constructive comments, honesty, understanding my connection to my writing and story, while helping me gain an objective point of view.

Our siblings Maxine, Philip, Michael, Susie, Beulah, and Paul. Surviving a family crisis and all the challenges required you all to step up with your love, support, and skills. You were all resilient under adversity, so dependable and helped us cope with whatever we were presented with.

Our nieces, nephews, cousins, friends, colleagues, and clients: this for sure was a village who helped us get to a healthy place. Rob Eisen, a rare kind of friend who showed up for us. We could rely on you to support us, at just the right time, in just the right way. Hilton Weinberg, Hilt, Steve's other brother, a lifelong friend, who has an abundance of generosity, love, caring, and hugs. A friend who everyone should have in their lives. Carolyn Tucker, you never hesitated to respond to being there for me or my family when we asked. You stayed supportive in the background always letting me know I could truly depend on you and I did. Randi, your unwavering encouragement, and friendship throughout and your initiative when it came to ensure this book got published. I am so fortunate and grateful.

My mom Jocelyn, wise, empathic, compassionate, passionate, supportive, giving and forgiving, and so tenacious. I learned much from the way you lived your life. The Rose of Sharon tree reminds me of your true beauty.

My dad Colin, so intelligent, knowledgeable, worldly, peace loving and supporter of worthy causes. When it came to your family, you wore your heart and emotions on your sleeve. I gained my love of books and reading from your example. You would be so proud of how all our lives turned out.

Josh and Gabi. The two people in my life I love beyond anything, forever. You dealt with our crisis and challenges in the best way you both could. I have seen that you both can do anything you set your mind to. You both live your lives with integrity, compassion, empathy, respect, and tolerance. Always support each other.

Stephen. All your traits and characteristics I was so attracted to when we were so young have proven to be most challenging and complicated. However, you have always had my back, encouraged and supported me in everything I have undertaken, enabled me to be my independent self, and in your own way have been an extremely loving husband and father. You have come a long way my determined friend and now, with our furry babies Hallie and Millie, we share the most peaceful and committed stage of our life.